Abbey Theatre Amharclann na Mainistreach
presents

LAY ME DOWN SOFTLY

BY **BILLY ROCHE**

WORLD PREMIERE

Lay Me Down Softly by Billy Roche was premiered by the
Abbey Theatre, at the Peacock, on 14 November 2008.

The Abbey Theatre gratefully acknowledges the financial
support from the Arts Council/An Comhairle Ealaíon

ABBEY THEATRE

Amharclann na Mainistreach

NEW WRITING SPRING 2009

Marble
By Marina Carr
Directed by Jeremy Herrin
10 February – 14 March
At the ABBEY
WORLD PREMIERE

Ages of the Moon
By Sam Shepard
Directed by Jimmy Fay
3 March – 4 April
At the PEACOCK
WORLD PREMIERE

Only an Apple
By Tom Mac Intyre
Directed by Selina Cartmell
21 April – 30 May
At the PEACOCK
WORLD PREMIERE

NEXT AT THE PEACOCK
La Dispute
By Pierre Marivaux
Translated by Neil Bartlett
Directed by Wayne Jordan
9 January – 7 February
ABBEY PREMIERE

Booking Áirithintí 00 353 1 87 87 222 www.abbeytheatre.ie

Lay Me Down Softly
By Billy Roche

The play is set in the early 1960s, somewhere in Ireland.
There will be one interval of 15 minutes.

Cast (in order of appearance)

Theo	Gary Lydon
Peadar	Lalor Roddy
Dean	Barry Ward
Junior	Joe Doyle
Lily	Aisling O'Sullivan
Emer	Ruth Negga

Director	Wilson Milam
Set and Costume Design	Ferdia Murphy
Lighting Design	Paul Keogan
Music and Sound Design	Philip Stewart
Fight Director	Paul Burke
Company Stage Manager	Tara Furlong
Deputy Stage Manager	Elizabeth Gerhardy
Assistant Stage Manager	Clare Howe
Voice Director	Andrea Ainsworth
Casting Director	Holly Ní Chiardha
Hair and Make-up	Val Sherlock
Photography	Colm Hogan
Graphic Design	Red Dog

This production has been licensed by arrangement with
The Agency (London) Limited, 24 Pottery Lane, London W11 4LZ
email info@theagency.co.uk

The Abbey Theatre wishes to thank RTÉ Television for its support of new writing.

Special thanks to Stephen Kavanagh, Ronnie Woods, Arbour Hill Boxing Club; James Stewart, Nash's Mineral Waters; Ray Lakes, Austin Carruth, Stephanie Ryan and to the National Fairground Archive, UK for the use of the cover illustration.

Please note that the text of the play which appears in this volume may be changed during the rehearsal process and appear in a slightly altered form in performance.

Billy Roche Writer

Billy's plays, performed at the Abbey Theatre, include *On Such As We, The Cavalcaders* and *The Wexford Trilogy.* He began his career as a singer/musician, forming *The Roach Band* in the late seventies. His first novel, *Tumbling Down*, was published by Wolfhound Press in 1986. His first stage play, *A Handful of Stars* was staged at the Bush Theatre in 1988. This was followed by *Poor Beast in the Rain. Belfry* completed this trilogy at the Bush Theatre. All three plays, directed by Robin LeFevre, became known as *The Wexford Trilogy* which was performed in its entirety at the Bush, the Peacock and the Theatre Royal, Wexford. His fourth play *Amphibians* was commissioned by the RSC and performed at the Barbican.

Billy wrote the screenplay for *Trojan Eddie* which was directed by Gillies MacKinnon and starred Stephen Rea and Richard Harris. He has been Writer-in-Residence at the Bush and Writer-in-Association with Druid and the Abbey Theatre. His book of short stories, *Tales from Rainwater Pond,* was published by Pillar Press and his recently revised version of *Tumbling Down* is published by Tassel Publications. A screenplay based on his short story, *Table Manners*, is currently in production, directed by Conor McPherson.

As an actor Billy has appeared on stage in *The Cavalcaders* (Abbey Theatre and Royal Court), *A Handful of Stars* (Bush Theatre), *Poor Beast in the Rain* (Andrews Lane Theatre), *Aristocrats* (Hampstead Theatre), *The Grapes of Wrath* (Storytellers) and *Amphibians* (Tin Drum Theatre). His film work includes *Strapless, Trojan Eddie, Saltwater* and *Man About Dog.*

CREATIVE TEAM

Wilson Milam Director

Wilson's work at the Abbey Theatre includes *Defender of the Faith* and *On Such As We*. His UK and Ireland theatre credits include *Swimming With Sharks* (Vaudeville), *Othello* (Shakespeare's Globe), *Santa Land Diaries* (Birmingham Rep), *Harvest, Fresh Kills* (Royal Court), *Flesh Wound* (Royal Court/Galway Arts Festival), *Chimps* (Liverpool Playhouse), *True West* (Bristol Old Vic), *Mr. Placebo* (Traverse), *A Lie of the Mind* (Donmar), *The Lieutenant of Inishmore* (RSC/Barbican/Garrick), *The Wexford Trilogy* (Tricycle/UK tour), *Hurlyburly* (Peter Hall Company at the Old Vic/Queens), *Bug* (Gate, London) and *Killer Joe* (Traverse/Bush/Vaudeville). US credits include *Three Changes* (Playwrights Horizons, NY), *Poor Beast in the Rain* (Matrix, LA), *The Lieutenant of Inishmore* (Atlantic/Lyceum/NY), *Closer* (Berkeley Rep), *Bug* (Woolly Mammoth, Washington DC), *Killer Joe* (Next, Chicago; 29th St. Rep/Soho Playhouse, NY), *Pot Mom* (Steppenwolf), *The Caine Mutiny Court-Martial* (A Red Orchid, Chicago), *Skeleton* (Shattered Globe, Chicago) and *Witness to Temptation* (American Blues, Chicago). Other work includes *Much Ado About Nothing* (RADA) and *Doctor Who: Scream of the Shalka* (BBC1).

Ferdia Murphy Set and Costume Design

Ferdia's work at the Abbey Theatre includes *The School for Scandal* and *True West* (both of which won him a nomination for Best Set Designer at the Irish Times Theatre Awards 2006), *The Burial at Thebes, The Recruiting Officer, Henry IV Part I, Ensuite* and *A Quiet Life*. He was nominated for Best Design at the Theatre Management Association (UK) Awards 2007 for *Dancing at Lughnasa* at the Lyric Theatre, Belfast. He was recently made an Honorary Scenographer by OISTAT (International Organisation of Scenographers, Theatre Architects and Technicians) at PQ07 in Prague. Last year Ferdia made his production design debut on the feature film *Porcelain*. Other work includes *Don Gregorio* (Wexford Festival Opera), *Knots* (CoisCéim), *Amadeus, Making History* (Ouroboros), *Shooting Gallery, Blasted* (Bedrock Productions), *Dinner with Friends* (Gúna Nua), *Macbeth, Tales from Ovid, Richard III, Mutabilitie* (Theatreworks), *Blown* (Theatre Royal, Plymouth), *True West, The Blind Fiddler* (Lyric Theatre, Belfast), *Passades* (Operating Theatre), *The Chance, Dealer's Choice* (Prime Cut), *The Consul, Inside Out* (Cochrane, London), *Sweeney Todd* (Bridewell, London), *In the Dark Air of a Closed Room* (Loose Canon), *Playing from the Heart, Rudolf the Red* (The Ark), *Devotion, Bumbugs and Bees* (TEAM), *Top Girls, Dolly West's Kitchen, Interludes, The Triumph of Love, The Dispute, Camino Royale* (Samuel Beckett Centre) and *Alternative Miss Ireland VI-IX* (Olympia). He trained at Central Saint Martin's College of Art and Design, London.

Paul Keogan Lighting Design

Paul's work at the Abbey Theatre includes *The Resistible Rise of Arturo Ui, Big Love, Romeo and Juliet, Woman and Scarecrow, Julius Caesar, The School for Scandal, Homeland* (also set design), *The Electrocution of Children, Amazing Grace, Living Quarters, Making History, The Map Maker's Sorrow, Cúirt an Mheán Oíche, Mrs Warren's Profession, Eden, Bailegangáire, Down the Line, The Wild Duck, The Cherry Orchard, Portia Coughlan* and *Heavenly Bodies.* Born in Ireland, Paul studied drama at Trinity College Dublin and Glasgow University. His lighting design work includes *The Taming of the Shrew* (Royal Shakespeare Company), *Tartuffe* (Playhouse, Liverpool), *Intemperance* (Everyman, Liverpool), *Harvest* (Royal Court), *Blue/Orange* (Crucible, Sheffield), *Born Bad, In Arabia We'd All Be Kings* (Hampstead, London), *The Walworth Farce* (Druid), *The Deep Blue Sea, Performances, The Gates of Gold, Festen* (Gate Theatre), *La Musica, Titus Andronicus* (Siren Productions), *Quay West, Blasted, Far Away* (Bedrock Productions), *Chair, Angel Babel* (Operating Theatre), *Catalyst* (Rex Levitates /National Ballet of China Beijing), *The Makropulos Case* (Opera Zuid, Netherlands), *The Lighthouse* (Cantiere Internazionale d'Arte, Montepulciano, Italy), *Snegurochka, The Mines of Sulphur, Susannah, Pénélope, Don Gregorio, Der Silbersee, Rusalka, Transformations* (Wexford Festival Opera) and *The Wishing Well* (Kilkenny Arts Festival). His lighting and set design work includes *The Sugar Wife* (Rough Magic), *Trad* (Galway Arts Festival), *The Hairy Ape* and *Woyzeck* (Corcadorca), *Chair, Here Lies* (Operating Theatre), *Ballads, The Rite of Spring* (CoisCéim), *The Massacre @ Paris* (Bedrock Productions) and *Shutter* (Siren Productions). Paul is an associate artist of the Abbey Theatre.

Philip Stewart Music and Sound Design

Philip's work at the Abbey Theatre includes *Terminus, A Number* and *The Big House.* As a freelance composer he has contributed music to a broad spectrum of genres including theatre, dance, documentaries and short films. He has developed a long-standing relationship with Hatch Theatre Company and created original music and sound design for their critically acclaimed production of *Further than the Furthest Thing.* His sound design featured as part of *Paranoid* an experimental theatre piece by RedBear Productions which premiered at this year's Dublin Fringe Festival. His music recently featured on RTÉ in April as part of its dance season special, *Dance on the Box.* He studied composition at Trinity College Dublin under Donnacha Dennehy and Roger Doyle.

Paul Burke Fight Director

Paul's work at the Abbey Theatre includes *The Resistible Rise of Arturo Ui, Big Love, Romeo and Juliet, Julius Caesar, True West* and *Fool for Love.* Other theatre credits include *American Buffalo, A View from the Bridge* and *Sweeney Todd* (Gate Theatre). Current film and television work includes *The Tudors, Heist, Calibre* and the forthcoming feature film, *Savage.* Paul is a member of the Equity Stunt Register.

CAST

Joe Doyle Junior

This is Joe's first time working at the Abbey Theatre. He trained at the Gaiety School of Acting and the Power House School of Music. Film and television credits include *Raw, Heartbeat, Smiles* and *Another Faith*.

Gary Lydon Theo

Gary's work at the Abbey Theatre includes *A Whistle in the Dark, The House, Translations, The Cavalcaders* and *Conversations on a Homecoming*. Other theatre work includes *The Cripple of Inishmaan* (National Theatre, London), *The Wexford Trilolgy* (Tricycle Theatre), *Poor Beast in the Rain, A Handful of Stars, Belfry, The Wexford Trilogy* (Bush Theatre), *Same Old Moon* (Nuffield Theatre, Southampton), *The Normal Heart, Young Europeans* (Project Arts Centre), *Pygmalion* (Gate Theatre), *The Boker Poker Club, Trumpets and Raspberries, The Fire Raisers, What the Butler Saw, Fool for Love* (Wexford Arts Centre), *The Playboy of the Western World, Sive, The Tinker's Wedding* and *The Well of the Saints* (Druid). Television credits include *Pure Mule, The Clinic* for which he won an IFTA (Irish Film and Television Award) for Best Supporting Actor in Television 2005 and 2006, *Sinners, Fergus's Wedding, Sunday, On Home Ground, Bramwell, Seaforth, The Wexford Trilogy, Hard Cases, The Bill* and *Bergerac*. Films include *Small Engine Repair, The Country, Leprachauns, Last September, Ordinary Decent Criminal, The Hunted, Michael Collins, Nothing Personal* and *Strapless*.

Ruth Negga Emer

Ruth's work at the Abbey Theatre includes *The Crucible, The Bacchae of Baghdad, The Burial at Thebes, Duck* (Out of Joint / Royal Court co-production), *Doldrum Bay, Lolita* (in association with The Corn Exchange) and *Sons and Daughters*. Other work includes *Oedipus Loves You, Amy the Vampire and Her Sister Martina* (Pan Pan), *The Playboy of the Western World* (Druid), *Titus Andronicus*, for which she won an Irish Times Theatre Award for Best Supporting Actress (Siren Productions) and *Súile Eile* (Fluxus Dance Company). Ruth was nominated for an Olivier award for her performance in *Duck* in 2003. Television and film credits include *Love is the Drug* (RTÉ), *Colour Me Kubrick, Stars, 3Minute 4-Play, Breakfast on Pluto*, nominated for Best Supporting Actress at the Irish Film and Television Awards 2007 and *Isolation* nominated for Best Actress at the same awards. Ruth's most recent television work includes *Criminal Justice* and *P.A.'s* for BBC. Ruth graduated from the Samuel Beckett Centre, Trinity College Dublin in 2002.

Aisling O'Sullivan Lily

Aisling's work at the Abbey Theatre includes *The Cavalcaders, Famine, The Honeyspike, On the Inside/On the Outside, Silverlands, The Winter Thief, Away Alone, The Corsican Brothers, The Power of Darkness* and *The Murphy Initiative*. Other theatre work includes *The Playboy of the Western World* (Druid) for which she won an Irish Times Theatre Award for Best Supporting Actress, *Crestfall* (Gate Theatre), *The Duchess of Malfi* (RSC), *Miss Julie* (Haymarket), *The Maids* (Young Vic), *Vasa* (Albery Theatre), *Mutabilitie, The Cripple of Inishmaan* (National Theatre, London), *Hysteria* (Duke of Yorks), *The Seagull* (Thelma Holt tour), *Slavs* (Hampstead Theatre) and *The Playboy of the Western World* (Almeida). Films include *The Actors, The One and Only, The Announcement, The American, The War Zone, The Butcher Boy* and *Michael Collins*. Television credits include *The Clinic,* for which she won an IFTA (Irish Film and Television Award) for Best Actress in Television 2007, *Me and Mrs Jones, Shockers, The Wyvern Mystery, Life Support, Cracker* and *Runway One*.

Lalor Roddy Peadar

Lalor's work at the Abbey Theatre includes *Observe the Sons of Ulster Marching Towards the Somme, In a Little World of Our Own,* for which he won an Irish Times / ESB Theatre Award for Best Actor, *Freedom of the City* and *The Tempest*. Other theatre work includes *The Lonesome West, John Bull's Other Island, Paradise, The Weir* (TMA Best Actor nomination), *Over The Bridge, A Doll's House* (Lyric Theatre, Belfast), *Hard To Believe* (Bickerstaffe), *Pentecost, Convictions, Gibraltar Straits* (Tinderbox), *Place of the Pigs* (Prime Cut), *Measure for Measure, Shadows, King Baby* and *Amphibians* (RSC). Film and television credits include *Boy Eats Girl, The Chosen, Pulling Moves, Peter The Great, All Things Bright and Beautiful, Circle of Deceit, Schizophrenic City, Lanes of Five, Between the Lines, Brinalaugh* and Steve McQueen's film, *Hunger,* winner of the Camera D'Or, Cannes Film Festival.

Barry Ward Dean

Barry's work at the Abbey Theatre includes *A Whistle in the Dark, A Quiet Life* and *Down the Line*. Other theatre work includes *Buddleia* (The Passion Machine), *Far Away* (Bedrock Productions), *Take Me Away* (Rough Magic, Heidelberg, Edinburgh, Bush Theatre), *The Lieutenant of Inishmore* (National Theatre, London), *Sive* (Druid Theatre), *The Playboy of the Western World* (Liverpool Playhouse) and *Monged* (Fishamble). Film and television credits include *Family, Plotlands, Lipservice, Sunburn, The Claim, Watchmen, The Bill, City of Vice, Silent Witness* and the award-winning *Danger! High Voltage*.

Give a dramatic
gift this Christmas

Whether you're buying for family, friends
colleagues or clients, a gift for the Abbey Theatre
is sure to entertain.

**Gift vouchers from €30, gift subscriptions from
€42 or gift memberships from €125 available
from the Box Office on 01 878 7222 or online at
www.abbeytheatre.ie**

Fáilte go hAmharclann na Mainistreach, amharclann náisiúnta na hÉireann

Osclaíodh doirse Amharclann na Mainistreach ar Shráid na Mainistreach ar an 27 Mí na Nollag 1904, le W. B. Yeats agus Bean Augusta Gregory mar stiúrthóirí. Ba iad a réamhtheachtaithe ná Amharclann Liteartha na hÉireann agus Cumann Drámata Náisiúnta Frank agus Willie Fay. Ar an 31 Mí Eanáir 2006 rinneadh an chuideachta seo a dhíscaoileadh agus bunaíodh cuideachta nua, Abbey Theatre Amharclann Na Mainistreach, a reáchtálann an amharclann anois. Níor tháinig aon athrú ar bheartas ealaíne Amharclann na Mainistreach go fóill agus cuimsíonn sé na spriocanna seo a leanas:

- Chun infheistíocht a dhéanamh i scríbhneoirí agus in ealaíontóirí nua Éireannacha mar aon le hiad a chur chun cinn

- Chun clár bliantúil de drámaíocht Éireannach agus idirnásiúnta a sholáthar atá éagsúil, tarraingteach agus nuálach.

- Chun réimse leathan custaiméirí a mhealladh is a ghníomhú agus chun eispéiris spreagúla, a thugann orthu teacht ar ais, a sholáthar

- Chun timpeallacht oibre bhríomhar a chruthú a sholáthraíonn cleachtas scothdomhanda ar ud ár ngnó

I 1925, thug Saorstát nua na hÉireann fóirdheontas bliantúil neamhghnách d'Amharclann na Mainistreach, agus tháinig sí ina céad amharclann fóirdheonaithe stáit i dtíortha an Bhéarla. Coinníonn ar An Chomhairle Ealaíon, mar aon lenár gcuid cairde ár bpatrúin agus sibhse, ár lucht féachana, tacaíocht a thabhairt dár gcuid oibre.

I 1951, rinneadh damáiste do bhunfhoirgnimh Amharclann na Mainistreach de bharr dóiteáin. Athlonnaíodh Amharclann na Mainistreach go dtí Amharclann na Banríona. Cuig bliana déag cothrom an lae sin anonn, ar an 18 Iúil 1966, bhog Amharclann na Mainistreach foirgneamh nua, a dhear Michael Scott, ar an láthair chéanna.

I Meán Fómhair 2006 d'fhógair an Rialtas go mbeadh comórtas dearaidh idirnáisiúnta ar siúl chun ionad buan nua a chruthú d'Amharclann na Mainistreach, a bheidh suite ar Ché Sheoirse i mBaile Átha Cliath. I nDeireadh Fómhair 2007 fógraíodh an coiste moltóireachta don chomórtas.

Idir an dá linn, thugamar faoi chlár athchóirithe agus uasghrádaithe d'fhonn cur leis an eispéire as dár gcuid ealaíontóirí agus daoibhse, a lucht féachana. Chuimsigh sé seo an t-athchumrú radacach, ar cuireadh fáilte fhorleathan roimhe, in halla éisteachta Amharclann na Mainistreach.

Go raibh maith agaibh as bheith linn don léiriú seo. Tá súil againn go mbainfidh sibh taitneamh as an seó agus tá súil againn nach fada eile arís go mbeidh sibh inár gcuideachta in Amharclann na Mainistreach.

Welcome to the Abbey Theatre, Ireland's national theatre

The Abbey Theatre opened its doors on Abbey Street on 27 December 1904, with W. B. Yeats and Lady Augusta Gregory as its directors. Its precursors were the Irish Literary Theatre and Frank and Willie Fay's National Dramatic Society. The company originally traded as the National Theatre Society Limited. On 31st January 2006 this company was dissolved and a new company established, Abbey Theatre Amharclann Na Mainistreach, which now runs the theatre. The artistic policy of the Abbey remains unchanged and incorporates the following ambitions:

- Invest in and promote new Irish writers and artists
- Produce an annual programme of diverse, engaging, innovative Irish and international theatre
- Attract and engage a broad range of customers and provide compelling experiences that inspire them to return
- Create a dynamic working environment which delivers world best practice across our business

In 1925, the Abbey Theatre was given an annual subsidy by the new Free State, becoming the first ever state-subsidised theatre in the English speaking world. The Arts Council of Ireland/An Chomhairle Ealaíon, along with our friends, patrons, benefactors and you, our audience, continues to support our work.

In 1951, the original buildings of the Abbey Theatre were damaged by fire. The Abbey re-located to the Queen's Theatre. Fifteen years to the day later, on 18 July 1966, the Abbey moved back to its current home, designed by Michael Scott, on the same site.

In September 2006 the Government announced that an international design competition would be held to create a new home for the Abbey, to be located at George's Dock in Dublin. In October 2007 the jury for the competition was announced.

In the meantime, we have undertaken a programme of refurbishment and upgrade to enhance the experience for our artists and for you, the audience. This included the radical and widely welcomed reconfiguration of the Abbey auditorium.

Thank you for joining us for this production. We hope you enjoy the show and look forward to welcoming you again soon to the Abbey.

Board
Bryan McMahon (Chairman), Catherine Byrne, Tom Hickey, Olwen Fouéré, Suzanne Kelly, Declan Kiberd, Dr Jim Mountjoy, Eugene O'Brien, Maurice O'Connell, Lynne Parker, John Stapleton

Executive

Fiach Mac Conghail	Director
Declan Cantwell	Director of Finance and Administration
Aideen Howard	Literary Director
Sally Anne Tye	Director of Public Affairs
Tony Wakefield	Director of Technical Services and Operations

Join us

The Abbey Theatre's **Friends, Patrons, Platinum Patrons** and **Corporate Supporters** make a real difference to what we can achieve. Their support helps us produce world-class theatre on the Abbey and Peacock stages, and allows us to invest in and nurture new Irish writers, directors, actors and designers.

Please **join us** – with your support the Abbey Theatre can have an even greater impact. We offer memberships with a range of benefits **from €125** and many opportunities for corporate involvement.

Please call Oonagh Desire, Head of Development, for more details on 01 887 2286. For further information please see www.abbeytheatre.ie

LAY ME DOWN SOFTLY

Billy Roche

Characters

THEO
PEADAR
DEAN
JUNIOR
LILY
EMER

Setting

The play is set in the early 1960s, somewhere in Ireland. We are
in a boxing booth in Delaney's Travelling Roadshow. A ring is
erected in a marquee tent and there is a raised dais of sorts at
the back wall with benches for the bystanders. The tent shows
signs that it was once a magnificent edifice. A small table and
chair are positioned close to the ring. A large sign reading 'ALL
COMERS' looms overhead. There are two flaps that open up
onto the green area outside – one on the far end of either side
wall. There are a few steps leading up to a covered-in wooden
kiosk with a turnstile for the punters. 'The Academy' is
emblazoned in back-to-front writing above the entrance. There
is a rough wooden floor with tufts of grass growing up through
it in places. A heavy punchbag dangles down. Through the flaps
and the odd chink in the tent's canvas we snatch a glimpse now
and then of the other fairground attractions – lights around the
Rifle Range perhaps, and the corner of the Merry-Go-Round
and whatnot.

*This text went to press before the end of rehearsals and so may
differ slightly from the play as performed.*

ACT ONE

*Lights rise on the boxing booth. It is Wednesday morning and
DEAN, in a lather of sweat, is skipping close to the punchbag.
PEADAR is working inside the ring, dismantling the ropes and
testing their durability and looking underneath the ring for
replacements, etc. THEO is busy inside the wooden kiosk. The
benches are stacked on top of each other out of the way.*

THEO (*off*). Peadar, you might take a look at this aul' turnstile
for us out here when you get a chance, will yeh?

> PEADAR *is an over-the-hill ex-boxer who moves with the
> grace and poise and quiet dignity of a man who has nothing
> left to prove.*

PEADAR. Yeah, right… Why, what's wrong with it?

> THEO, *glasses on, enters with account books and a cashbox,
> etc. He is a big, rough, fierce, commanding middle-aged
> man.*

THEO. Nothin', as far as I can see. Lily says it was stickin' on
her last night. The punters had to climb in over it, she said.
Which was all very well until some big fat one got stuck and
put the kybosh on it all. They had to come in through the
side flap in the end I believe.

PEADAR. I was wonderin' why they were comin' in that way.

THEO. Huh…? What's goin' on?

PEADAR. His nibs…! He wants them tightened, he said.

THEO. Tightened?

PEADAR. Yeah. (*He grimaces.*)

DEAN (*quenching his thirst*). They're too loose, Theo. I mean,
there's no what-do-you-call-it in 'em – snap. And that floor
is scandalous too, I don't mind tellin' yez.

THEO. The floor as well be God, hah.

PEADAR. Madison Square Garden he wants.

DEAN. What?

THEO. Put a bit of powder on it, why don't yez. Till we all have a bit of a dance.

PEADAR. I know.

THEO. Hah? (*He sings 'The Blue Danube'*.) 'Da da da da da da da da da...'

DEAN. Did yeh see your man last night, Theo?

THEO. 'Da da da da da da da da da...'

DEAN. He went down like a bag of shit, boy. Oh, the tingle! (*He snaps out a punch*.)

PEADAR. Yeah, we all saw that, didn't we, Theo?

THEO. Witnessed it. We all witnessed it.

PEADAR. That's it. That's the very word I was... how-would-you-put-it-now... searchin' for.

THEO *is sitting at the table, books open.*

DEAN. What's that supposed to mean?

PEADAR *hisses and turns away.*

He was givin' me impudence. Theo. 'You're not hurtin' me,' says he to me when I hit him the first time. 'I can't feel a thing,' says he. 'No?' says I. 'No,' says he like that. 'Nothin'.' 'Here,' says I to him when the time was right, 'Feel this.' Wham...! Teeth and blood flying in all directions. Oh dear me...

PEADAR. A terrible stupid thing to do if you ask me.

DEAN. Come again.

PEADAR. No need for it.

DEAN. That's a matter of opinion... Anyway, it's good for business.

PEADAR. That's just the point, it's not.

DEAN. Not what?

PEADAR. Good for business.

DEAN. Yeah well, I've a reputation to think of, pal – unlike the rest of yez. So let the word go forth. That right, Theo?

THEO. Huh?

DEAN. I say let it be known, boy.

THEO. Yes, powder for little twinkle toes.

DEAN. How's that?

THEO (*menacing*). Yeh what?

PEADAR. Was your man alright after, Theo?

THEO. Yeah, he was alright. A bit groggy, that's all.

DEAN (*cockney accent*). Groggy? Not 'alf! I'll say. Eh?

THEO. I got Junior to drop him home in the truck.

DEAN. All heart, boy.

THEO (*licking his fingers and counting the money*). That's me all over. Theodore Delaney. Blessed are the blessed for they shall be humble and pure at heart. One hundred and fourteen smackers. Henceforth and forthwith! (*He writes it into his ledger.*)

PEADAR. And was he alright did he say?

THEO. Yeah... As I say... he was groggy.

DEAN (*taking off the old fellow's tipsy swagger*). I wish you a Merry Christmas and a Happy New of the Year.

JUNIOR *enters, a lame, handsome young man with a laconic nature and the slow heartbeat of a slightly washed-out prizefighter.*

Junior there'll back me up on that now, won't yeh, Junior?

JUNIOR. What's that?

DEAN. Those ropes.

JUNIOR. What about them?

DEAN. I say they're too slack.

> JUNIOR *makes a face.*

> And the floor. Tell him what you said about the floor, Junior. What you said to me the other day there. Go ahead.

> JUNIOR *sighs and shakes his head.*

THEO. Any sign of Lily yet?

JUNIOR. Yeah, she's talkin' to Rusty out there.

DEAN. *Again!* You'd want to keep an eye on that fella, Theo. That's a whoremaster goin' around, that lad is. I wouldn't mind but they say he's hung like a horse too. (*He neighs.*) Junior, gives us a hand here, will yeh. (*Indicates the set of boxing gloves.*)

PEADAR. How was your man last night after, Junior?

JUNIOR (*going to help* DEAN *with the gloves*). Who's that?

PEADAR. The aul' lad?

DEAN. He wasn't an aul' lad, Peadar.

JUNIOR. Alright, I think.

DEAN. He was about your age.

JUNIOR. I mean, I just dropped him off, like.

DEAN. You didn't go in for the sup of soup then, no?

JUNIOR. I did in me hat. I dropped him at the door and got out of there. 'Cause he was fairly shook up, yeh know.

DEAN. Yeah well, now he knows. Tie it tight, will yeh.

JUNIOR. Hold still then. A rough-enough part of town too.

DEAN. The Bowery, be Jaysus, hah...? Or old Skid Row! (*He laughs – a distinctive sound...*) That's better... Yes, hung like a horse, he is. (*He punches the heavy bag.*) He has

women all over the place, yeh know? – Rusty! Some of the
lads were sayin' he has two or three on the go at any given
time.

PEADAR. I heard that alright.

JUNIOR. It's a good job he's not good-lookin' – he'd be
dangerous.

DEAN. He has it where it counts though, lads. (*He whistles to
indicate.*)

PEADAR. I suppose. When all's said and done, like!

DEAN. That's what I say.

Laughter.

THEO (*in a fury*). Are you goin' to take a look at that aul' turnstile out there for me or not, yes or no? – like I asked yeh.

PEADAR. What?

THEO. Instead of fuckin' around with that thing for him there.
The ropes were alright the way they were. Lave them be, be
fucked. You'll be puttin' powder on the floor next.

PEADAR. Junior, come on, you're better at this lark than me.

JUNIOR. What lark?

PEADAR. The turnstile is stickin', apparently.

JUNIOR. Yeah?

THEO. The whole thing dismantled, be Jaysus. For what? Bull-
shit!

PEADAR (*muttering*). Here we go again.

JUNIOR. What?

THEO. Never mind mutterin' there at all.

PEADAR. Yeh what?

THEO. I said less of your aul' guff there.

JUNIOR. Probably just needs a drop of oil or somethin'.

THEO. Tightened!

JUNIOR. Show us.

THEO. One of yez do it. You don't need the two of yez to... I mean, what am I runnin' around here anyway – Butlin's Holi-fuckin'-day Camp or somethin'?

PEADAR (*coming away from there*). Alright.

JUNIOR (*bewildered*). What?

THEO. Two of them to put a drop of oil on a bit of an aul' rag and what-do-you-call-it... I don't know.

PEADAR. Alright, I said. Now lave it, will yeh.

THEO. Yeh what?

PEADAR. Jesus Christ tonight, man, give it a rest, will yeh.

THEO. There's enough people restin' around here already as it is, I think, without me startin'. Yes, Butlins Holiday fuckin' Camp you must all think you're in, the lot of yez.

THEO *blatantly watches* PEADAR – *who is tempted to mimic him – going about his business.* JUNIOR *checks the turnstile and then goes to get his toolbox from under the boxing ring as* LILY *enters.*

LILY. Mmn... I love that smell. Sweat and dust and leather. And somethin' else, what is that? (*She teases the air.*)

PEADAR. Rope.

JUNIOR *chuckles nervously.*

THEO (*suspicious*). What?

DEAN. Well, Lily, how's Rusty gettin' on out there?

LILY. Rusty?

DEAN. Yeah. Is he alright?

LILY. Rusty's alright, yeah, why?

DEAN. Nothin'... We were just... yeh know... talkin' about him here. We were just sayin' what a popular fella he is and that.

LILY. Yeah?

DEAN. Yeah. Don't yeh think?

LILY. I don't know... I suppose so.

DEAN. What?

Pause as LILY *throws* JUNIOR *a dirty look.*

THEO. What have you got for me?

LILY (*putting different bags of money on the table*). These are mostly last night's now. The Rifle Range, the Bumpers, the Swing Boats, the... which one is that? (*She reads the sticker.*) Oh yeah, the Helter Skelter.

THEO. Which one's Rusty's?

LILY. The Bumpers... He owes yeh two nights he said: last night and the night before.

THEO. Oh, I know that. Don't worry about that... Let's see... what's in here...? Yeah... Forty-eight, forty-nine... And what's that? Mmn... (*He looks in a ledger.*)

DEAN. Did little Ernie tell yeh about your man winnin' all before him at the Rifle Range last night, Lily?

LILY. Yeah.

DEAN. Hit the bull's-eye every time, boy. Bing bang boom... Must be in the FCA or somethin', lads – this fella. Cleaned the place out so he did – every doll and teddy bear and ornament in the shop. Hard set to carry it all home, I believe.

LILY. I know. I had to follow him down the lane and buy it all back again, sure.

DEAN. Yeah...? Yeah, well, let's just hope he don't turn up again tonight. Little Ernie'll be gettin' the file out, I think.

DEAN *mimes Ernie filing the sights on a gun which he then fires, missing his imaginary target by a mile and making comical chicken noises.*

THEO. Yeh know, I've been checkin' back through the books here, Peadar, and – no matter where I put this joker – the takin's are always down.

PEADAR. Rusty?

THEO. Yeah. Bumpers, Helter Skelter, Chair-O-Planes, whatever. Down. And I'm not talkin' nickels and dimes eider.

PEADAR. Yeah?

THEO. Yeah. And he lets it build up over a period of a few nights before he hands it over, in spite of the fact that I told him – several times actually – to give it to me every day, every mornin'. Lookin' back through the books there, I see he's down again there now.

PEADAR. How much?

THEO. I don't know... A good few quid a day anyway. I mean – a day, like! A week maybe, yeah, I might tolerate, but...

PEADAR. A day? Jesus!

THEO. Huh?

LILY. Business hasn't been that brisk lately though, Theo, yeh know. Over the past few weeks, I mean... I mean there were nights there when there was hardly anyone around.

THEO. I'm allowin' for that... He's takin' the piss.

THEO *rises purposefully, taking off his glasses and pocketing them.*

DEAN. Do you want me to go over and have a word with him or anything for yeh, Theo?

THEO. You? A word? For me...? I don't think so.

DEAN. No?

THEO *shakes his head.*

LILY. Now Theo, don't go jumpin' the gun. I mean, just talk to him, see what he has to say for himself... Theo... Theo, do you hear me...? Peadar, talk to him, will yeh.

PEADAR *throws his arms in the air, helplessly.* THEO *is already going out through the lower flap with* PEADAR *at his heels.*

DEAN. Well, what do you know? Big red Rusty's on the rack. Yup out of that!

He laughs and follows the others outside. LILY *goes as far as the flap to watch them go and then she sighs and stands to disdainfully watch* JUNIOR *hobbling to and fro, oil can and toolbox in hand.*

JUNIOR. What...? He asked me where you were and I told him, that's all. I mean... (*He shrugs.*) I warned you anyway.

LILY. What? I'm not supposed to talk to anyone? I'm supposed to just... what? Bury my head in the sand or somethin'?

JUNIOR. I warned yeh and I told yeh... Time and time again I told yeh.

LILY. I mean, do you know what it's like? Have you any idea what it's...

JUNIOR. And Peadar told yeh too.

LILY. ...like... lumbered with that big lummox. With his jigsaws. I mean, jigsaws – hangin' on the wall like they were the *Mona Lisa* or somethin'!

JUNIOR. So don't say you never knew. You knew.

LILY. Watching me and checking up on me all the time...

JUNIOR. Every time he sends me lookin' for yeh, it's the same old story.

LILY. Jesus, I can't even...

JUNIOR. I find you lurkin' in the shadows or hangin' out in someone else's trailer or somewhere.

LILY. ...talk to anyone but he's...

JUNIOR. I mean, it stands to reason that sooner or later he's goin' get...

LILY. And what do you mean, I knew? Knew what?

JUNIOR. You knew what would happen to Rusty.

LILY. What?

JUNIOR. The same thing that happened to what's-his-name. Do you remember him? What's-his-name? With the... eh... with the teeth?

LILY. Yeah, I remember him. Of course I remember... Young Luke.

JUNIOR. Yeah. Luke!

LILY. What about him?

JUNIOR. He didn't look so good the last time I saw him, let's put it that way. I mean, he was...

LILY. He was what?

JUNIOR. Luke didn't look so good.

LILY's face shadows with regret as JUNIOR stuffs the toolbox, etc. back under the ring again.

LILY. I hope Rusty beats the shit out of him. I really do... Just for once yeh know I'd like to see someone just... yeh know...

JUNIOR. Yeah, right.

DEAN (*returning*). Junior, yeh missed it. A peach, boy.

JUNIOR. Yeah?

DEAN. Oh Lort! Stop...! 'Are you accusin' me of something?' says Rusty to him, reachin' for a wrench. Bang... End of story! If that jaw's not broke I'll eat somebody's hat. A beaut, boy!

LILY. Where's he now?

DEAN. On the ground.

LILY. Theo, I mean?

DEAN. I don't know... Ransackin' a trailer I'd say... Well, Peadar, what did yeh think of that then? A beaut?

PEADAR *enters with the confiscated wrench which he stores in the toolbox under the ring.*

PEADAR. A lucky punch.

DEAN. Yeah, right… I'd say that jaw is gone, Peadar, would you? Hah? It's definitely fractured anyway – at least.

PEADAR. Sore enough, I'd say.

DEAN. I'll say. Not 'alf! Eh…? Bang. Get that stitched. Oh dear!

JUNIOR. No resistance, no?

PEADAR *shakes his head.*

DEAN. None that you'd notice anyway. Whoosh…

LILY *winces with disappointment at the very thought of it all.* THEO *enters, holding up a wad of notes.*

Whahoo!

THEO (*to* PEADAR). A tidy little nest egg.

PEADAR. Where?

THEO. Under the floorboards.

DEAN. Slimy bastard.

THEO. He was savin' up, by the looks of it.

DEAN. Yeah, for what though? Sexual innuendoes? (*He chuckles – that distinctive sound again.*)

THEO. Yeh what?

DEAN. I beg your pudding.

THEO *sizes* DEAN *up and then, acting baffled, he gathers all the bags of money and the books and ledgers and the cashbox together, etc., and prepares to leave.*

THEO. Let the word go forth.

DEAN. Oon Theo… Let it be known, boy. Henceforth and forthwith!

THEO exits. PEADAR rubs his tired eyes and crosses the floor. DEAN – overexcited – hits him a nifty punch in the solar plexus. PEADAR doubles over in pain.

PEADAR. Oh, yeh bastard, yeh.

DEAN. Oh yes!

JUNIOR. Hey, take it easy there.

DEAN. What's up with you?

JUNIOR. What's up with me? I'll tell yeh what's up with…

DEAN. Yeh what?

They sort of square up to each other. PEADAR roughly steps between them.

PEADAR (*to* DEAN). One of these days, boy!

DEAN. What…? Peadar, where he is!

DEAN kisses PEADAR on the forehead and turns his attention to the bag, banging it furiously. PEADAR rebuffs JUNIOR's assistance and, slightly winded, he goes about his work. JUNIOR stands to look at LILY. She seems filled with a wild, new-found admiration for DEAN as she watches him perform. Lights down.

Lights rise. Late afternoon. PEADAR is sitting ringside on an old wooden crate, drinking tea which he pours from a teapot that has been brewing on a banged-up Primus stove. The ropes around the ring are back in place, except for the side facing the audience which is still an open space. DEAN enters.

PEADAR. How's she doin' out there?

DEAN. Alright, I think. He's showin' her his jigsaws now: a real treat for her.

PEADAR. 'Snowflakes and Daffodils', hah?

DEAN. No – 'A Windy Street in April' these days.

PEADAR. Moved on?

DEAN. Looks like it… Many round tonight?

PEADAR. Yeah, it's lookin' up, mind yeh.

DEAN. Yeah?

PEADAR. Mmn… (*He looks at his list.*) There's two lads want to fight each other. A three-rounder. Two brothers. Or first cousins, rather.

DEAN (*sniffing a milk bottle*). What's the beef?

PEADAR. Search me. They just want to fight each other, that's all… Oh, and that big lad's comin' down from the north again to have another smack at you. What's-his-name – you fought him before – Crowley.

DEAN. Oh right. Big awkward-lookin' bollix.

PEADAR. That's the one… Thinks he was diddled the last time. You were holdin' back, right?

DEAN. Big time.

PEADAR. He's in for a bit of a land then so.

DEAN. Afraid so… I'm not refereein' anything tonight now, right?

PEADAR. Theo'll take care of that, I'd say.

DEAN. Good. Because it sort of takes the look off things when I do it.

JUNIOR *enters with a box of supplies/groceries. He places the box on the edge of the ring and doles out a few things – popcorn and cigarettes for* DEAN, *a Crunchie and lemonade for* PEADAR, *a brown bag of luncheon sausage for himself, a bottle of milk and a bag of sugar and a packet of tea, etc., which* PEADAR *piles into their own little wooden supply box.*

DEAN. We'll rope in Gunga Din there too, yeah?

PEADAR. Junior? Oh yeah… You'll take the odd one, won't yeh?

JUNIOR. What's that?

PEADAR. I say you'll take the odd one? (*He mimes fisticuffs*.)

JUNIOR. The odd one…? Yeah. No bother.

DEAN. Earn his keep.

JUNIOR. I see Paddy Hickey the bookie pullin' in there a minute ago – in his Merc!

DEAN. Well for him… Go out and tell him you'll take three to one on me knocking out your man in the first – see what he says to that. Yahoo!

Slight pause.

PEADAR. How's the foot?

JUNIOR. Alright.

PEADAR. No worries?

JUNIOR *silently reassures him.*

There's tea there, Junior – if yeh want.

JUNIOR. Huh?

JUNIOR *pours himself a mug of tea and sits on the ringside. DEAN lights up a cigarette and watches him, somewhat contemptuously. LILY enters.*

LILY. Damaged goods – that young one is, if you ask me.

PEADAR. How do you make that out?

LILY. I don't know… She's too… (*She searches for the right word – 'watchful' or 'intense'*.)

PEADAR. I like her.

LILY. Ah!

PEADAR. What?

LILY. Pfff… (*She waves away his opinion*.)

JUNIOR. Who's that?

DEAN. Theo's daughter – Emer – turned up out of the blue.

JUNIOR. What, while I was…

DEAN. Yeah. After what? Fifteen or sixteen-odd years nearly?

PEADAR. About that alright – a little more in fact, I'd say.

LILY. What's she wantin', is what I'd like to know.

PEADAR. How do you mean?

LILY. I mean, what's she after – what's she lookin' for, like?

PEADAR *shrugs*.

DEAN. As long as she's not here to fill your shoes, Lily, what harm, eh?

LILY. Ha!

DEAN. How did she get here anyway?

LILY. Hitched apparently… Ran away by the sounds of it.

DEAN. Yeah? 'Snowflakes and Daffodils', hah?

LILY. Oh stop! And then they wonder why I'm… I don't know.

DEAN. Ah no, credit where credit is due now – 'A Windy Street in April', I like that one – hangin' on the wall! Hah? (*He laughs.*)

LILY *throws him a dirty look*.

LILY. What did yeh get? Everything and anything! (*She peers into the box of groceries.*)

DEAN. I should think so too – gone half the fuckin' day.

JUNIOR. Yeh what?

LILY. Ovaltine? (*She looks towards* PEADAR.)

DEAN. Yeah – Rip Van Winkle there!

DEAN *chuckles*. PEADAR *half-heartedly throws an old mitt at him.*

PEADAR. Shut up, you…! The last time I saw her she was only about two or three years of age, yeh know. Or two-and-half maybe. Her mother brought her to see us in Carrig-on-Suir – one winter's day.

DEAN. Yeah? Did yeh dandle her on your knee, Peadar?

PEADAR. No, I put her on the Merry-Go-Round actually. I can still see her now – holdin' on for dear life with one hand, big thing of candyfloss in the other. (*Sings*.) 'Lady of Spain, I adore you...' Rain drippin' from the canopy down onto her furry red hood and she lookin' up at it that way. Plop plop plop plop plop...

JUNIOR. Yeah?

PEADAR. Mmn... (*He mimes her protecting the candyfloss from the rain and insinuates, 'plop plop plop...'*)

JUNIOR *smiles.* LILY *scowls and shakes her head at the foolishness of it all.*

LILY (*going into the kiosk*). Oh, that reminds me, Junior, that aul' Merry-Go-Round is actin' up again too. I mean, it's goin' and all the rest of it but, there's no music out of it... I must get you to...

JUNIOR. It's already done – this mornin'.

LILY (*off*). Fixed?

JUNIOR. Yeah – early this mornin'.

DEAN. There's service for yeh, boy... (*He dabs out his cigarette and plants the butt behind his ear.*) I wouldn't mind dandlin' her on my knee now, lads, would you? Hah? Oh Lort. Stop.

PEADAR. Hey.

DEAN. What?

PEADAR. That'll do yeh.

DEAN. You're right there, it would.

PEADAR. What?

DEAN. Do me.

DEAN *chuckles as* LILY *returns with a cushion to sit on.*

You've a lovely big back on yeh, Lily. Did anyone ever tell you that?

LILY. No.

DEAN. Well, yeh have… I love backs, boy.

LILY. Do yeh now?

DEAN (*twinkling*). I do. I'm partial to a bit of front too, mind yeh – from time to time, like.

LILY *bends over him and pinches some of his popcorn.*

LILY. What about the back of the hand – do you fancy a bit of that, no?

DEAN *weaves out of the way as* LILY *flings the popcorn into his face.* LILY, *smirking, goes to sit beside* JUNIOR *where, much to his discomfort, she helps herself to a slice of his luncheon sausage. Meanwhile,* DEAN *winks at* PEADAR *behind her back.*

JUNIOR (*to* PEADAR). I never even knew Theo had a daughter.

LILY. He don't like to talk about it. Do he, Peadar?

PEADAR. No.

DEAN. Why not, Lily? Too painful?

LILY. Too expensive more like it – the stingy bastard! (*She imitates his stingy face and mimes foraging in her palm for coins, etc.*) 'I told him to give it to me every day, every mornin'… yah yah yah…'

They all laugh – even JUNIOR *in spite of himself – as* THEO *and* EMER *enter.* EMER *is a young, wild, waif-like creature with a surly straight-as-a-dye way about her, in spite of an underlying sense of wounded uncertainty.*

THEO. There yez are. Alright?

PEADAR. Yeah.

DEAN. No bother.

LILY. Why wouldn't we be?

JUNIOR. Huh?

THEO. What are yez laughin' at?

PEADAR. Nothin'.

THEO. Yeh what?

PEADAR. Nothin'. We were just... yeh know... havin' the craic here, like.

THEO. Yeah...? About what?

PEADAR. Hard to explain really.

THEO. Try me.

    PEADAR, *under pressure, looks to the others for support.*

LILY. We were just talkin' about your jigsaws here and for some unknown reason they all thought it was very funny.

THEO. Yeah?

PEADAR. Don't mind her.

DEAN. I like the jigsaws. Hangin' on the wall and all? Good idea!

LILY. What do you think, Emer?

EMER. I don't know – a bit daft if you ask me.

LILY. I rest my case.

THEO. Mmn... I'm outnumbered here I think... Anyway, Emer, Peadar you already met, and Lily. And Dean, of course. Or 'Killer Deano' as he likes to call himself. And that's Junior there.

EMER. What does he do?

THEO. Junior? Whatever.

EMER. Huh?

THEO. He fixes things. He gives us a hand here too now and again, don't yeh, Junior?

JUNIOR. Yeah.

DEAN. When we're stuck.

THEO. Junior was a great welterweight one time: a contender. He hurt his foot then and that was the end of that. What happened, Junior – Achilles tendon or somethin', was it?

JUNIOR. Yeah, the old heel went on me.

DEAN. He's a ballet dancer now.

JUNIOR *shies away from* EMER*'s intense gaze.*

THEO (*proudly, re: the boxing booth*). 'The Academy.'

EMER *looks around the place. Behind her back* LILY *lips, 'How long is she staying?' to* THEO, *who just shrugs his shoulders in return.*

EMER. Any animals here?

THEO. Animals? No.

EMER. No horses or anything, no?

THEO. No.

LILY. We're not a circus, yeh know.

EMER. Never said you were...! So what are yeh anyway, a sort of a sideshow or somethin'?

LILY. A sideshow!

PEADAR. Good girl, Emer.

EMER. What?

EMER *disappears into the kiosk.* LILY *eyes* THEO *while she's out of sight.*

THEO. I always avoid usin' that... phraseology meself, but... 'sideshow' I suppose would be eh... would be... one way of...

EMER (*off*). Yeh don't have a fortune-teller by any chance, do yeh?

THEO. We do. Sadie.

DEAN. Yeah and if you see her, Emer, you might ask her what's goin' to win the three-thirty tomorrow, will yeh?

Laughter as EMER *returns into view.*

EMER. What?

THEO. Don't mind them. And before you ask me, we've no freaks either. We've a couple of weirdos hangin' around alright, but… definitely no freaks.

DEAN. Not countin' Ellen, that is.

THEO. Oh stop… Ellen was our unofficial bearded lady for a while there – well, a bit of meg on her, like.

Disapproving sounds all round.

What…? Look at Peadar, actin' all innocent there. You said it too, mate – about her… Ellen left in a huff… Anyway, you'll see all of that for yourself after. Mind you, it might not appeal to you, of course – if you're anything like your mother anyway.

EMER. I don't know about that. Mammy told me she always loved all this. As a matter of fact I'd say she'd still be here only you two bailed out and left her in the lurch.

THEO. Who told you that?

EMER. She told me herself.

THEO. What, that I left her in the lurch?

EMER. Yeah. In Cappoquin or somewhere.

THEO. Cappoquin? (*He looks to* PEADAR.)

PEADAR. Dungarvan actually.

THEO. Yeah well, Joy wasn't really cut out for this life, yeh know. Goin' from town to town and all – one aul' field after another.

LILY. Unlike me, that is.

THEO. Huh?

LILY. A big strappin' heifer. Ha!

THEO. No, I mean we didn't have our own show on the road that time or anything. It was real hand-to-mouth stuff. I mean... It didn't really suit her, yeh know... She actually told you I bailed out?

EMER. Yeah, why?

THEO. I don't know. I just thought she might have told yeh I was dead or somethin'... noble like that.

EMER. No. She said she woke up in this little hotel one rainy mornin' and you two were gone. She waited there for two or three days, she said, and then she ran out of money.

THEO. For a start, it wasn't rainin' that day and I left her enough money. But sure, Peadar went back and everything – to check on her. Didn't yeh, Peadar – a few days later?

PEADAR. Yeah.

EMER. I think she was convinced there was another woman involved.

THEO. Ah now, the other woman wasn't for a while after – a good while after... (*To* PEADAR.) Big Angie! Oh!

The two men silently recoil in horror.

Did she mention the first time we met? No...? She didn't go into all of that, no?

LILY. Oh please... Do us all a favour, will yeh! (*She exits.*)

THEO (*calling after her*). What...? That was long before I even met you... She hates me tellin' this yarn... Is she gone there, yeah...? The first time I saw Joy, she was strollin' through the fairground, right? – alongside her brother John. You should see this fella, lads. A big bull's head on him. And hands like two shovels. And shoulders! Jaysus...! A giant, Peadar, wasn't he? In every sense of the word.

PEADAR. A fairly big man alright.

THEO. Strong as an ox too! Is he still alive, yeah?

EMER. Uncle John? Yeah. We live with him in fact...

THEO. Yeah?

EMER. ...unfortunately.

THEO. He'd be fairly hardy now too, of course. He used to come into the boxin' booth now and then, but none of us had the balls to take him on. So we decided to pay him off. Every night – a little backhander to just… yeh know… go away! Remember the first night, Peadar? Oh, be the Lort Jaze tonight!

PEADAR. Yeah.

PEADAR *indicates to himself – the short straw.* THEO *laughs and points and shrugs.*

THEO. Anyway, here he was, shufflin' from stall to stall this night, as I say, and there she was beside him. I swear you could nearly see through her she was that delicate-lookin' that time. She was like… I don't know… I was very nearly goin' to say 'glass' but that's probably not the right word… You've her complexion actually.

EMER. Thanks.

THEO. Huh…? So anyway as soon as I got a chance I asked her out – behind your man's back now, I hasten to add – to the pictures on our first date, in the afternoon – a matinée. (*He mimes his arm around her in the back row.*)

EMER. What was on?

THEO. Oh, I don't know. Some queer aul' yoke. We went to the seaside the next day – on bicycles. And another time we had a picnic – on a hill somewhere. Little sandwiches. No crusts. Flask of tea… (*He plays at eating and drinking.*) A yoke-me-bob spread out and all… Yeh know?

DEAN. No, but we get the gist.

THEO. What…? (*Indicates* PEADAR.) He wasn't there… Porcelain…! Anyway, when it was time for us to move on again I asked her to come with me and she said she'd love to, only she was half-afraid of what big John might do. So that night I went to her house and slipped in the back way and made my way through the maze – the scullery and the living room and the little parlour, as she called it. Up the stairs then – past your man's room and everything with the door ajar.

Eventually I found her and while the big fella slept, the pair
of us crept hand-in-hand down the stairs to Peadar, who was
waiting outside in the aul' pick-up truck, and away we went
in the moonlight – the three of us! Bamp bamp…!

EMER. What if he woke up?

THEO *makes a face – 'too bad for someone if he did'.*

THEO. So she's livin' back there with him these days you tell
me, yeah?

EMER. Uh-huh. The two of us are.

THEO. Oh right.

Awkward pause.

PEADAR. We should never have left her there if you ask me.

THEO. Accordin' to you, we shouldn've brought her with us in
the first place.

PEADAR. No, we shouldn't, but we shouldn't have left her
there eider.

THEO. Yeah well… We did… Or I did, I should say…! Big bad
John, hah? 'Fee fi fo fum.'

*He makes the sound of John tramping heavily down the
stairs and laughs.* EMER *is not amused.*

Here, come on… Let her see yeh spar – you two… Your
mother used to ring the bell and that. Do you want to…

He moves the table and chair ringside and gives PEADAR
*the bend to retrieve the bell from beneath the ring. He then
guides* EMER *towards the table and chair where the bell
now stands. She tries it for size, the bell ringing out
triumphantly.*

Meanwhile, JUNIOR *and* DEAN *have climbed into the ring.*
PEADAR *is in* JUNIOR*'s corner,* THEO *in* DEAN*'s, as they
slip on the gloves, etc.* THEO *steps out into the centre of the
ring to act as referee and he gives* EMER *the bend to ring
the bell.*

During the action above, LILY *has entered, licking a big ice-cream cone as she jealously spies* EMER *sitting at the table.* DEAN *and* JUNIOR *go to it, clinching and punching and grunting,* THEO *stepping between them now and then calling, 'Break' and 'Mind the heads' and 'Box', etc.*

LILY (*crying out to* THEO *when the time is right*). By the way, little Ernie thinks we've got a pro on the premises.

Slowly the whole thing winds down as one after the other of them realises what she has just said.

THEO. A pro?

PEADAR. What did she say?

JUNIOR. We've a pro on the premises.

DEAN *hits* JUNIOR *a last smack during all of this.* JUNIOR *retaliates so that there is a little flurry of activity during it all,* PEADAR *stepping in between the two of them.*

DEAN. How does he know he's a pro?

LILY (*still licking*). I don't know. Someone recognised him, I suppose.

THEO. Where is he now?

LILY. Ernie?

THEO. The pro?

LILY. Don't know... The Rifle Range or somewhere.

THEO. Shit... Peadar, go take a look, will yeh.

DEAN. I'm not gettin' in the ring with no pro, I'm tellin' yeh that now for nothin'.

THEO (*calling after* PEADAR *as he exits*). Have a word with him, Peadar... See what he wants.

EMER. I thought it said 'All Comers.'

DEAN. Yeh what?

EMER. 'All Comers.' The sign?

DEAN. Yeah I know, but you don't expect a pro to turn up though.

EMER. No?

LILY. Maybe he's a has-been.

DEAN. Don't matter – a pro's a pro.

THEO. Let's not panic now. Find out who he is and what he wants first.

LILY. I couldn't see anyone that looked like a pro. But then again I've never seen a pro so... how would I know?

THEO. Could be just hangin' around.

DEAN. I wouldn't mind but I'm after atin' a hape of popcorn and everything.

THEO. This could cost me dearly.

DEAN. I mean, I'll fight anyone, like, but I draw the line at a pro.

LILY. Could be excitin' though... Yeh know, the challenge.

DEAN. Yeah I know, but...

LILY. Huh?

THEO *and* DEAN *and* LILY *are standing near the flap now, looking off into the distance.* JUNIOR *is sitting on the side of the ring, legs dangling,* EMER *close by.*

EMER. I thought you were the best.

JUNIOR. Thanks.

DEAN *overhears this and scowls at her. Under* LILY*'s suspicious gaze,* EMER *winks and smiles up into* JUNIOR*'s face when* DEAN *turns away. Lights down.*

Lights rise. Darkness is beginning to fall. EMER *is giving*
JUNIOR *a hand to set out the benches – on the raised dais
behind the ring and also around the front and sides.* PEADAR
is busy wrapping bandages on DEAN's *hands.* DEAN *is togged
out in his fighting gear – nicks and vest and boots and a robe
with 'Killer Deano' on the back of it. The ring is fully roped at
this stage.*

DEAN. Make them fairly tight now.

PEADAR. They're alright, they're tight enough. Where's that…
scissors… Junior, did yeh see the… eh… Oh, it's alright, I
got it.

JUNIOR. What?

PEADAR. It's alright, don't worry about it.

LILY (*entering*). Junior, Theo told me to tell yeh you're to get the
bench out of our place and the two chairs by the window.
Sadie said you can use her long wooden form too. We're goin'
to be inundated by all accounts. Emer, when you're done there
you can sort out the tangle under the ring. I mean, if the fire
officer comes down and sees that, he'll shut us down forthwith… I mean to say there's glue and everything in there.

EMER, *dreading the prospect, makes a face to* JUNIOR *who
indicates that he is going to get the chairs and bench, etc.*

Peadar, did Theo do anythin' about the cops?

PEADAR. Yeah, that's all sorted I think. As long as there's a
local club involved.

LILY. He squared it, did he?

PEADAR. Yeah – as far as I know.

LILY *goes into the kiosk.*

DEAN. So tell me about this fella again, Peadar?

PEADAR. What else can I tell yeh? Joey Dempsey, a good
welterweight. A citeóg. Hard. Fast. A good mover. Packs a
punch in either hand. Thirty-two or -three or thereabouts

now. His best days behind him, you might say, but
nevertheless...

DEAN. Nevertheless what?

PEADAR. What? Where's that tape?

LILY (*from the kiosk doorway*). Emer... (*She gives her the bend
to come closer.*) The tape's inside there in the drawer,
Peadar... (*To* EMER.) I wouldn't get me hopes up about that
fella if I was you.

EMER. How do yeh mean?

LILY. Trust me.

> PEADAR *passes through and disappears into the kiosk to
> look in the drawer for the tape.*

EMER. Ah no, we're gettin' on fairly well, like.

LILY. Yeah? In what way?

EMER. I don't know... He showed me around the place and
that earlier on. The Hall of Mirrors and the Ghost Train and
the Helter Skelter and all. We cut across the field then past
the Shrine to the railway station there. We had a bit of a
laugh, yeh know – behind the milk churns and that.

LILY. I bet he didn't try anythin' though, did he? No. That's
what I thought. And he won't eider. Thinks he got it for
stirrin' his tea, that lad... Peadar, someone's goin' to need to
man that flap there tonight because if I'm swamped here the
sly ones'll slip in that way.

PEADAR (*coming back out*). Yeah, I'll keep an eye on that.

LILY. Stick Emer on it there... Never mind makin' faces at all
there, girl. If you're goin' to hang around here you'll have to
learn to pay your way and earn your keep the same as the
rest of us.

EMER. I'm not sayin' anythin'.

LILY. Yeh what...? I don't know what she's sayin' half the time.
The fighters'll be comin' in that way – (*The other flap.*) I
presume, Peadar, yeah?

PEADAR. Yeah... Usually anyway.

LILY slips into the kiosk again as JUNIOR *enters, bench in one hand, two chairs in the other.* EMER, *raging, sticks her tongue out at* LILY *behind her back, much to* JUNIOR's *delight and* PEADAR's *amusement.*

DEAN. Junior, you fought this fella a couple of times, what more can you tell me about him?

JUNIOR. Nothin' really. Just more or less endorse what Peadar was sayin' earlier on there. I fought him twice. We drew the first time and I won the second. I was supposed to fight him again only for this. (*His foot.*) You talked to him and all, Peadar, did yeh?

PEADAR. Yeah. Theo told me to offer him a good few quid, but... he wouldn't bite. He promised his uncle, he said.

JUNIOR. Oh right.

EMER (*clearing the underbelly of the ring*). What's his uncle got to do with it?

JUNIOR. Dean gave his old uncle a hidin' here the other night.

DEAN. I didn't give him a hidin', Junior. I gave him a couple of slaps.

JUNIOR. Your man was a bit... groggy after it.

DEAN. And he wasn't an aul' fella either. He was about Peadar's age there.

EMER. So he's lookin' for revenge, is he?

JUNIOR. Somethin' like that.

EMER. Deadly.

DEAN. I mean to say if the shoe had've been on the other foot, Peadar, he'd've done it to me, yeh know.

PEADAR. Yeh reckon?

DEAN. Are you coddin' or what?

EMER. How much will he get if he wins?

JUNIOR. Twenty guineas.

EMER *whistles, impressed.*

I know.

PEADAR. You make sure to keep your left foot outside his right all the time, Dean, do you hear me? And the left hook is your best bet with a fighter like that. Just, yeh know, snap it out there every chance you get.

DEAN. Yeah, I know, you told me all that.

PEADAR. Yeah well, don't forget it.

DEAN. I need a leak.

PEADAR. What...? Don't loosen those... bandages.

DEAN *exits through the flap.*

JUNIOR. Did anyone think about tryin' to run Joey Dempsey out of here altogether?

PEADAR. There's a rake of them in it – cousins and what not...! I didn't say nothin' to Dean but your man reckons he's goin' to go to town on him – to teach him a lesson. He intends comin' back the night after next too he says, which, let's face it – if he keeps that up anyway – is goin' to force us to move on prematurely. I wouldn't mind but this field is already paid for and everything... You're goin' have to handle your man from the north tonight, Junior. What's-his-name... Crowley!

JUNIOR. Yeah?

PEADAR. Mmn... I mean... (*He shrugs.*)

THEO *enters.*

THEO. Peadar, get us out the aul' megaphone there, will yeh. If we're goin' to lose money we might as well shout it from the rooftops.

PEADAR. Your man Dempsey said he doesn't want it announced.

THEO. Pity about him. Go ahead... Lily, is that turnstile workin' now?

LILY (*off*). Yeah. I think so.

THEO. Make sure it is there, will yeh. Where's the other fella?

PEADAR is encouraging EMER to go in under the ring for the megaphone.

JUNIOR. He's beyond there.

THEO goes to the kiosk and returns with a big bottle of Lucozade which he swigs from.

LILY. Have you managed to have a word with that young one yet?

THEO. About what?

LILY. How long she's stoppin' and all the rest of it.

THEO. No, I didn't.

LILY. Well, do you not think yeh should, like? Where's she sleepin' tonight anyway?

THEO. Sadie's. I told her she could move into young Luke's aul' trailer in the mornin' if she's willin' to clear it out.

LILY. Luke's?

THEO. I don't see why not. It's an extra pair of hands as far as I'm concerned… What?

LILY. She's goin' to bring us trouble, I know it.

THEO. How do you make that out?

LILY. I heard her in the phone booth at the end of the lane earlier on there, talkin' to her mother. Shoutin' into the mouthpiece she was, a right little rip if you ask me, slammed the phone down and everything. I mean, that's all I need now, her mother showin' up here too, turn this thing into a family affair. Before you know it I'll be on the side of the road meself.

THEO. Don't go blowin' this out of proportion now.

LILY. Yeah well, let me tell you, mister, I've plenty of alternatives if that does come to pass.

THEO. What do you mean?

LILY. You know what I mean. I've alternatives or invitations or whatever, plenty of them, and I'll use them too if I have to.

THEO *grabs her arm and drags her near.*

THEO. Now you listen to me.

LILY. You listen to me, you mean.

THEO. You try any more of that shit around here and I swear to God I'll...

LILY. Yes, you listen to me, mate.

THEO. I mean it. If I catch yeh or see yeh or even smell yeh doin' anything like that again, I'll fuckin' well...

LILY. Well, get shut of her then. Before she takes you for everything. I mean, for all you know...

THEO. For all I know, what?

LILY (*breaking free*). Ah!

LILY *disappears inside the kiosk.*

THEO (*calling after her*). For all I know, what, I said.

LILY (*off*). Wise up, will yeh...! I'm goin' to need some petty cash here too.

THEO. Yeh what?

LILY. Look, it's alright, I'll ask Rusty.

THEO. Rusty! I thought I gave him his walkin' papers, no? Obviously not.

PEADAR. Are yeh right?

THEO, *with an air of wolf-like anger, turns to look at him.*

(*Testing the megaphone.*) HELLO... ATTENTION... HELLO... ERNIE, LEAVE YOURSELF ALONE THERE... That's grand...

THEO (*tetchy*). For fuck's sake... Give it here. (*He snatches it from* PEADAR.) You drive the truck, I'll... Emer, are you wantin' to come with us now or what?

EMER. No, I'll hang on here. Give Junior a hand.

THEO. I thought you said you wanted to come with us?

EMER. No... I don't.

> THEO *thinks about it, gives* PEADAR *the bend to follow and they exit,* PEADAR *trading a glance with* JUNIOR *as he leaves.* EMER *dons one of the boxing gloves for size.*

> Do you think Dean'll be able for your man tonight?

JUNIOR. Doubt it.

EMER. Serves him right then... Sadie tells me I'm goin' to live beside a river someday, yeh know: in a little cottage. Well, she didn't exactly say 'a little cottage', but... stands to reason...! And she said that I was born to kiss away the pain too, which, I may as well tell yeh here and now for nothin', is not like me at all, but that's what she said. And when I asked her about you, about your foot and that, she told me to tell yeh you're not to be leavin' your footprints lyin' around after yeh... (*She acts perplexed.*) I think there's somethin' goin' on between herself and little Ernie, yeh know. He peeped in a couple of times while I was there with her. I've cramped his style I think... (*She chortles.*) How did you hurt your foot to start with anyway?

JUNIOR. Skippin'.

EMER. Sore?

JUNIOR. At the time, yeah. It was like someone had just kicked me in the back of the leg. As a matter of fact I turned around to chastise the culprit, but...

EMER. Nobody there...? Just as well.

JUNIOR. Mmn.

> *Pause as she stares at him.*

> What else did Sadie say?

EMER. Oh, I don't know, the usual stuff: I'm headstrong, I'm this, I'm that, I'm the other... Oh, and she knew I was born on Christmas Day too. I thought that was fairly good; and

she mentioned the word 'Joy' at one stage which is in fact
my mother's name, so... All in all, like. I wonder if she
knows who's goin to win the fight tonight? I should have
asked her that, shouldn't I? Whoosh...

She moves in to box JUNIOR. *He instinctively covers up,
blocks her punches and manoeuvres around her, tangling her
up in clinches, etc., much to her delight and frustration.
Until he spies* LILY *watching it all from the kiosk and that is
when* EMER *tags him with a light shot to the jaw. He instinctively grabs her and draws her towards him roughly. Pause.
She gently touches his face and then in time she lightly kisses
the spot where she hit him as* THEO's *voice can be heard in
the distance, booming through the megaphone.* JUNIOR
steps shyly back away from her.

DEAN *returns and* EMER *takes off the glove and hands it to
him as he passes and then she slowly returns to her work.*
DEAN *wonders about it all as* LILY *moves out of view.*
DEAN *sits in the shadows and ruminates, as* JUNIOR
touches the spot where EMER *kissed him and softly smiles.*

THEO (*off, through the megaphone*). Don't miss this incredible
spectacle – the local welterweight Joey Dempsey will take
on the undefeated Dean Murphy in a five-rounder that prom-
ises to be a truly royal battle of the Titans. Come and support
your very own Joey Dempsey tonight in the boxing booth of
Delaney's Travelling Roadshow as he takes on the undefeated Dean Murphy. Yes, folks, tonight is the night in the
boxing booth of Delaney's Travelling Roadshow. Treat yourself and your family to a night out at Delaney's Travelling
Roadshow – Bumpers, Helter Skelter, a Ghost Train, the
Wheel of Fortune and a Rifle Range and many other fairground attractions, followed by the big fight in the Academy
Boxing Hall of Delaney's...

Lights down.

Lights rise. Night. The boxing booth is littered with cigarette
stubs and screwed-up betting slips and sweet wrappings and
paper and cans and bottles and discarded debris, etc. DEAN is
lying prostrate on a bench, his robe draped over him like a
blanket. PEADAR is kneeling beside him. JUNIOR is standing
close by. LILY and EMER are sitting on the steps leading to the
kiosk, drinking bottles of beer by the neck. THEO is fumbling
around inside the kiosk.

PEADAR. Dean... Dean... He's still dead to the world.

JUNIOR. Well, you did warn him.

PEADAR. I did, didn't I...? Several times actually... Dean...
    Dean...

THEO (*off*). Lily, where's the raffle money?

LILY. I have it here.

THEO (*entering*). How'd yeh do after?

LILY. Good... Well, for midweek, like. Did yeh fix Joey
    Dempsey up alright?

THEO. I did. Twenty guineas.

LILY. What did he say?

THEO. He said, 'Thanks very much, I'll see yeh Friday night.'

LILY. He's comin' back?

THEO. Yeah – the night after next... Is he still sleepin'?

PEADAR. Yeah. Dead to the world.

THEO. Give him a blast of the queer stuff there, one of yez...

PEADAR. I'd sooner see him comin' round of his own accord,
    to tell yeh the truth.

THEO. But sure he's not comin' round, is he? Get 'em out
    there, Junior, or we'll be here half the night.

    JUNIOR *searches under the ring for a little medical kit. He*
    finds the smelling salts and hands the container to PEADAR,
    who holds it under DEAN's nose.

LILY. I see Paddy Hickey the bookie there tonight too – in all his splendour. Did yeh see him, Emer...? No...? A real handsome-lookin' man with sort of distinguished grey hair and a lovely long overcoat on him...

EMER *shakes her head.*

Real sallow skin? Looks like a sheikh... Drives a Merc...! No...? Did you see him, Theo?

THEO. Who's that?

LILY. Paddy Hickey the bookie! Yum yum yum... (*To* EMER, *confidentially.*) He winked at me as I was goin' by. (*She demonstrates and chuckles.*)

THEO. Yeah, I had one of the boys put a fiver with him on this fella here goin' down in the second. Three to one. Very nice. Recouped some of my... Oh whist, he's comin' round... A bit of a stir anyway.

PEADAR. Dean... Dean... sit up for me now, me aul' son. Sit up, Dean... Dean... Look at me.

THEO. Well done with your man tonight, Junior – the fella from the north, I mean. Fair play to yeh!

JUNIOR. Thanks.

THEO. No great shakes, as it turned out.

JUNIOR. No.

THEO. I believe Wild Bill Hickok was back at the Rifle Range again tonight too. (*He turns to* LILY.) How much did yeh give him after?

LILY. Thirty bob. He hung on to a few things – for his niece and nephew, he said.

THEO. Well now, he'll be gettin' the bum's rush down that lane tomorrow night if he turns up here again because... You couldn't put up with that.

PEADAR. Good man, Dean, that's the style.

THEO (*leaning into* DEAN). Alright, Deano... Three to one I got... Yeah, you went down right on cue, boy, fair play to yeh.

PEADAR. Open your eyes, Dean. That's it. Open them wide for me now. Good boy… That's it.

DEAN. Where am I?

THEO. Where are yeh? Where *were* yeh would be more like it, I think.

DEAN. What?

PEADAR. You're alright.

DEAN. Everybody gone, yeah?

PEADAR. Yeah, they're all gone home to their beds.

DEAN. Yeah?

THEO. Yeah. As a matter of fact some of them are probably gettin' up now.

DEAN. Huh?

PEADAR. Stand up for me. That's it. You're alright… Are yeh alright?

DEAN. Yeah, a bit groggy that's all.

LILY. What's wrong with him?

THEO. He's groggy.

LILY (*scornful*). I mean, he didn't hit him that hard or anythin'.

PEADAR (*helping* DEAN *into his robe*). You're alright.

THEO. Remember the next time, Deano: left foot outside his right. Got that? Yeah?

DEAN. Yeh what?

THEO. Talkin' to the wall.

PEADAR. Take him across to the trailer there, Junior.

JUNIOR. Right.

JUNIOR *leads a dazed* DEAN *out through the flap and away.*

LILY. What ails him?

DEAN. I mean, your man was a pro, like, yeh know.

JUNIOR. I know.

DEAN. I mean to say that's... that's... ridiculous, like, yeh know.

DEAN *and* JUNIOR *are gone*.

LILY (*disgusted*). But sure he only tapped him from what I could see.

PEADAR. What are we goin' to do, Theo? I mean, we can't put Dean back in the ring with that fella.

THEO. I know. It's a pity because this place'll be jammed, I'd say. Even payin' out the twenty guineas there tonight now, I made a few bob on the transaction – between one thing and another, like! Imagine how well we'd do if we could beat your man. Clean up, boy!

EMER. Why don't yeh put Junior in there with him?

THEO. Junior?

LILY. Ha!

EMER. He beat him the last time, didn't he?

LILY. Yeah, he had two legs then though.

EMER. He says it's gettin' better. And he nearly destroyed the fella from the north there tonight.

LILY. Yeah – a waster!

EMER. How do you make out?

LILY. Look...

THEO. Lily's right! Joey Dempsey's a pro – or was a pro anyway. I mean, yeh can't put a fella with a limp in there with a lad like that. He'd kill him.

EMER. It's just a thought.

THEO. What?

LILY. No chance.

EMER *pouts*.

THEO. No, it's not a bad suggestion or anything. I mean, you're right to suggest it, like... What do yeh think, Peadar? I mean he's sparrin' pretty good these days.

LILY *makes a furious face behind his back.*

PEADAR. Yeah I know, but... We'll see.

THEO. Huh...? I'm goin' to tell yeh one thing, lads, but if I was ten years younger, boy.

EMER. Yeah?

THEO. Oh yeah, I'd have a go anyway... Ask Peadar. It wouldn't be pretty, but...

LILY. Yeah but you're not though, Theo, are yeh? I mean, let's face it.

THEO. Not what?

LILY. Ten years younger.

THEO. Isn't that what I'm sayin'. I'm not. But if I was is all I'm sayin'.

LILY. But sure what good is that? 'If I was'!

THEO. What?

LILY. I mean, you're not and that's all there is to it. And for all we know you never were.

THEO. Never was what?

LILY. I don't know... Good enough. Fit enough. Tough enough. I mean, he's a pro, like.

THEO. Believe you me, girl, I was good enough and tough enough once upon a time.

LILY. Ha!

THEO. What – to take on the likes of him?

LILY. Yeah well, we only have your word for that, haven't we?

THEO. Ask Peadar. He'll vouch for me. Not that I need anyone vouchin' for me or anythin'.

LILY. Where would we all be without Peadar? To vouch for us!

THEO. What...? Give me the raffle money.

She reluctantly hands it over.

Stubs.

She gives him the book of ticket stubs.

This is all in order here, I presume, yeah?

LILY. What do you think?

THEO. I'm thinkin' it better be. Otherwise you wouldn't be sittin' there suckin' on that thing there, would yeh?

She storms off, sulkily.

LILY (*as she exits*). Fuckin' prick!

THEO (*calling after her*). Very nice... Yes... Lovely... In front of...

LILY (*off*). Fuck off...! Bastard!

THEO. That's it, show your true colours... Nail 'em to the mast, why don't yeh.

EMER (*unaffected by it all*). So you were a fighter then too in your day, yeah?

THEO (*pacing to and fro like a wounded alpha*). Yeah, I was – since I was fifteen years of age. Contrary to what others might tell yeh... I mean, ask anyone. I came up the hard way, mate.

EMER. Yeah?

THEO. Yeah. Brought up by me grandfather and he reared me rough.

EMER. What did he do?

THEO (*testy*). Me grandda? He was a rag-and-bones man, why?

EMER. Just wonderin'.

THEO (*suspicious*). Yeah...? (*He studies her and softens.*) When I say he reared me rough, I mean... he was hard on

me. And me poor mother was too, God be good to her –
although she tried her best, I suppose. I was out doin' mes-
sages when I was seven years of age, sellin' newspapers
when I was ten and workin' full time by the time I was
twelve – right after me confirmation.

EMER. Where was your da?

THEO. He was missin' without leave. And yeah, I know: it runs
in the family – like wooden legs!

EMER. Did you ever track him down?

THEO. I didn't need to. I knew where he was.

EMER. Where?

THEO. East End of London. Runnin' a gym down there. As I
say, I went over there when I was fifteen years of age – goin'
on sixteen. Against me grandfather's wishes too, although he
slipped a few quid, fair play to him, into me top pocket as I
boarded the train. Caught the mail boat to London then
and… that was that: never looked back.

EMER. What was the name of the club?

THEO. 'The Old Emerald Isle.' Irish fighters mostly. Black fellas
too though and Welsh lads. All sorts. That's where I met
Peadar. He was a fighter and trainer at the time. Comin' to the
end of his fightin' career due to a hand injury. Me da wasn't too
pleased to see me eider, I don't mind tellin' yeh. Only for old
Cat Bergin he'd've sent me straight back. Cat convinced him I
had potential. Although how he came to that conclusion now
I'll never know. I was only a wet day in the place when they
pitched me against this big Welsh geezer by the name of Davis.
He nearly kilt me in the first two rounds, dancing around on the
balls of his toes and all that. Yeh know, real fancy sort of stuff,
jabbin' and hookin' and all the rest of it. Until Peadar there
pointed out his fatal flaw to me in the corner: he dropped his
right like this every time he threw a straight left. And that's
how I tagged him – with a cross. Wham. A bag of shit at me
feet! Me da doin' his nut at the ringside. Your man was one of
his risin' stars. Oh! (*He demonstrates the punch.*) Sickened!

EMER. Where did you sleep?

THEO. That night?

EMER. Every night?

THEO. Every night? Or most nights at any rate – in a dusty little room at the back of the gym. Bed, locker and a chair to hang me clothes on.

EMER. You didn't live with your father?

THEO. Are you coddin' me or what? He was shacked up with this big blonde one called Nancy at the time, who wasn't exactly over the moon about a little Irish knacker like me arrivin' unannounced at her doorstep. No, I slept at the back of the gym. Got up to all sorts of mischief too. Peadar there had to bail me out of more scrapes than little... The row with the pimp that time, Peadar!

THEO laughs as PEADAR shakes his head in memory.

EMER. And what about Nancy? Did she ever get to like yeh after?

THEO. She did. As a matter of fact, she got to like me very much... (*He grins as JUNIOR returns.*) Did you tuck him in, yeah?

JUNIOR. He's listenin' to the radio.

THEO. Yeah? Which station?

JUNIOR. Radio Éireann.

THEO. That should cheer him up no end. We'll clean this place up tomorrow, lads. Junior, see where she is, will yeh. I'm gone ahead over tell her.

JUNIOR. Yeah right, Theo.

THEO. Oh!

He doubles back and takes the two chairs which he loops his arms into, and he leaves, singing into the megaphone:

'Ireland Mother Ireland. *Ireland Mo Chroi*... Ireland Mother Ireland. *Macusla Mo Chroi*...' Ernie, what are you at out there?

THEO *is gone.* JUNIOR *hangs around for a while as*
PEADAR *puts the gloves and gear and medical kit, etc.*
away under the ring. EMER *rises and she tenderly takes*
JUNIOR'*s hand and they softly kiss and slowly exit together.*
PEADAR *lovingly watches them go and when they are gone*
he sits there on the edge of the ring, lights up a cigarette and
ponders it all. Lights down.

End of Act One.

ACT TWO

Lights rise. It is a sun-filled morning, Thursday. EMER *and*
PEADAR *and* JUNIOR *are sitting around the ring, cushions all
around and a basket and blanket spread out like a picnic. The
ropes are dismantled and lying in a heap on the ground. A small
pile of refuse sacks and boxes are piled by the flap. The place is
reasonably spick and span again, the benches all piled together
as before.*

PEADAR *is busy about the place and, during the following, he
breezes in and out of the tent: to lower the big punchbag down
and rummage under the ring for the gloves and mitts and skipping rope, etc., disappearing through the flap now and again
only to return with small weighing scales and a body ball and
other bits and pieces.*

JUNIOR *picks up a milk bottle, which he sniffs and tastes like a
wine expert.*

JUNIOR. *Daisy Day...* Don't tell me: we're in the midlands,
right? Just outside Bridgewater somewhere.

EMER *sort of cheers and applauds.*

...Now if it was *Milkmaid* we'd be in Stoneyville.

EMER. What about Huntley Town?

JUNIOR. Eh... *Fireside Dairies*? No, *Avondale*, though. Am I
right?

EMER. Bang on.

JUNIOR *winks and taps his wily temple.*

One way of knowin' where yeh are in the world at any point
in time, I suppose.

JUNIOR. I suppose. Good as any.

EMER. Mmn…

They chuckle and hold hands.

What about you, Peadar, how do you tell where you are in the world from day to day?

PEADAR. I don't… I'm good and lost wherever I am.

EMER (*going to him and hugging him affectionately*). Aw…! Peadar!

PEADAR (*avuncular*). Works every time, boy.

LILY *enters, picking up scraps of paper and stuffing them into a refuse bag, etc.*

EMER. *Daisy Day*, Lily, where are we?

LILY (*lighting up*). I neither know nor care.

EMER *snickers as she silently offers* LILY *a cup of tea.*

EMER. Where are you from originally anyway, Lily?

LILY. A one-horse town called Knocknanoo.

EMER *looks to* JUNIOR *for the appropriate creamery.*

JUNIOR. Never heard of it, mate.

EMER. Tch!

LILY. That's half the problem.

EMER. Yeah? What's the other half?

LILY. Huh?

EMER. Sounds like a wood pidgeon, don't it. 'Knocknanoo…'

EMER *and* JUNIOR *laugh.* LILY *throws them a dirty look.* EMER *gags herself and giggles.*

Knocknanoo, Peadar – the milkiest milk in the world!

PEADAR. So they say.

LILY. *Rafferty's*, yeh mean.

EMER (*grimacing*). What?

LILY. I know, they couldn't even do that right... They own half
Knocknanoo – the Raffertys: creamery, bakery, public house,
the lot. Their oldest lad – Owen – took a great shine to me
one time. Tried everything under the sun, he did. I turned him
down and he blushed like a big baboon every time he passed
me in the street. I wouldn't mind but I could have been away
with it there, boy. But no, Lily married the bread man.

EMER. What was he like?

LILY. Seanie? He was fairly serious – set in his ways. I mean,
he knew well enough I wasn't happy livin' there but it never
even occurred to him to do anything about it.

EMER. How come?

LILY. Oh, I don't know... He didn't want to lose what he had, I
suppose. What he had! A brown coat and a book of fuckin'
dockets! Ha!

EMER. Seanie?

LILY. Mmn... Seanie Dunne – from Knocknanoo.

LILY *throws her eyes to heaven.*

JUNIOR. No children, Lily, no?

Slight pause.

LILY. No.

LILY *busies herself wiping a speck of ash from her blouse as*
EMER *throws* JUNIOR *a disapproving glance.*

EMER. What was on Rafferty's bottle? 'Rafferty's'?

LILY. A woman on her way to town – coat, scarf and basket.
The thing I liked about her though, was she always looked
like she might not be comin' back. We went within spittin'
distance of Knocknanoo about a year and a half ago there,
and I nearly cried when I saw that woman on her way to
town. She's on the bread wrapper too, by the way. She's on
nearly everything actually. That was the day, at least I think
it was the day, that I caught a glimpse of Seanie talkin' to
Sadie at her trailer door. And I thought, 'Well now, that's

novel, a man with no past worth talkin' about wants to know what the future holds in store for him.' Ha! I hid behind the Rifle Range until he was gone and then I went over to Sadie's to find all my belongings dumped on the threshold – all my stuff. And there was I, half-hopin' he'd come to put up a bit of a fight for me at least... (*She shakes her head and scoffs.*) He's with some other yoke now, I believe. Probably scrubbin' my Rayburn as we speak... (*Re: the rubbish.*) You can leave all that, Peadar, little Ernie's goin' to haul it all down to the end of the lane tomorrow sometime.

PEADAR. Did he say that, yeah?

LILY. Yeah.

PEADAR. I'll just dump it all outside here then, I think.

LILY. Whatever yeh like.

PEADAR – *under* LILY*'s scornful gaze* – *removes all the refuse from the boxing booth.*

EMER. Is Peadar a partner here or what, Lily?

LILY (*shakes her head and yawns*). A hired hand.

Across the way, PEADAR *bends to pick up a lost coin, which he duly spins.*

EMER (*calling out*). Toss yeh for it, Peadar.

PEADAR (*flips it, turns it, looks at it, pockets it and exits*). Hard luck.

EMER *chuckles sadly.*

EMER. I dare say Sadie wasn't exactly over the moon about that then, was she – all your stuff landed on her doorstep like that?

LILY. She made out like she saw it all comin'.

EMER. Probably did too – knowin' Sadie anyway... What did Theo say?

LILY. He said he's saddled with me now whether he likes it or not. Yeah!

EMER. Tch... Men, Peadar.

PEADAR (*passing*). What about them?

EMER. They're stupid.

PEADAR. That's a fact alright – where women are concerned anyway.

EMER. Peadar...! Where did you meet Theo in the first place, Lily?

LILY. His truck broke down up the road from me one day.

EMER. Oh right... (*She winks at* JUNIOR.) You weren't on your way to town at the time by any chance, were yeh?

LILY. I was, as it happens. And there he was, under the bonnet – sleeves rolled up and dirt on his face, callin' in to poor Peadar to let out the choke or somethin'. Before I knew it I was singing 'Adi Do Da Day'. Ha!

THEO *enters, sleepy-headed and cranky-looking.*

THEO (*re: the ropes*). What's goin' on here?

EMER. We're resting... Say 'Thank you, Emer, Junior and Lily.'

THEO. Yeh what?

She indicates the spick-and-span nature of the place which he silently acknowledges. She then pulls back the little curtain-like fringe beneath the ring and, with a discreet cough, guides his gaze towards the underbelly of the ring which is also in a tidy state.

Any sign of Deano yet?

PEADAR. Yeah, he's up and about and all.

THEO. Well?

PEADAR. Ah, yeh know?

THEO. Mopin' around?

PEADAR. That's it.

EMER. He's humbled… Lily was tellin' us about Knocknanoo here. Weren't yeh, Lily? How much she misses it and that.

THEO. What's there to miss? Nothin'.

EMER. What's there to what? The woman on her way to town, the one horse, the river…

THEO. She couldn't wait to get out of it, she told me.

EMER. The little streams and babbling brooks and all.

LILY. I must have been out of my mind then…

EMER. And Rafferty's Bar and Bakery.

LILY. …leavin' my lovely house and home – for this place! Jaysus!

EMER. I mean…

THEO. No one kidnapped yeh. Or what-d'you-call-it… twisted your arm or anythin'. That right, Peadar?

PEADAR *indicates to leave him out of it.*

LILY. What was I thinkin'?

THEO. Yes, no one forced yeh…! Oh here, while I think of it.

He hands her some money.

LILY. What's this?

THEO. The raffle money. Although accordin' to the stubs, you were two bob short.

LILY (*exiting*). Check the floorboards why don't yeh?

THEO (*calling after her*). One of these days, I will… I let her keep the raffle money.

EMER. Yeah?

THEO *gestures – 'all heart'.*

…Anyway, listen, we've some good news for yeh. Junior has agreed to fight Joey Dempsey tomorrow night. And not to worry: Sadie took one look at his palm and predicted triumph ahead.

THEO. Good. Unfortunately it's not his palm I'm worried about.

EMER. His foot is gettin' better too. Ain't it?

JUNIOR. It feels a lot better anyway.

THEO. Yeah? What brought that on?

JUNIOR. How do yeh mean?

THEO. Only the other day you were limpin' around the place like a one-legged sailor. Now all of a sudden you're wantin' to...

JUNIOR. No, it's just gettin' better, that's all. I mean it's... comin' round.

THEO (*suspicious*). Did you know about this?

PEADAR. What?

THEO. Junior takin' on your man tomorrow night?

PEADAR. Yeah.

THEO. Am I the last to know everything around here?

PEADAR. Usually. Here, get to work. (*He throws* JUNIOR *the skipping rope.*) Nice and easy does it now.

JUNIOR *rises, strips off and does a few warming-up exercises while* EMER *puts the flask and cups, etc., back into the basket.*

EMER (*re: the underbelly of the ring*). What do you think, Peadar?

PEADAR. I'll be struck off.

EMER. Bring on the fire officer. Come on down... Chu chu chu...

PEADAR *enjoys her sense of mischief.*

THEO. What are yeh goin' to do, Peadar, put him through his paces now or what?

PEADAR. Yeah – somethin' like that.

THEO. Good idea – a light workout now, a good sleep tonight and a bit of a warm-up tomorrow afternoon before the fight.

PEADAR. That's it.

JUNIOR *starts to skip*.

THEO. Good… Overhaul the ring… Nice… Do you hear that?

EMER. What?

THEO. He's to get some sleep tonight.

EMER (*slapping his hand*). The cheek of you. We're not all like you, yeh know.

THEO. Yeah, well, it saps the strength.

EMER. More than the strength in your case.

The distant tune from the Merry-Go-Round – a practice run perhaps – prompts EMER *to initiate a waltz with* PEADAR.

(*Singing.*) Lady of Spain, I adore you,
    Right from the first time I saw you…
    La la la la la la la la…
    Lady of Spain, I'm in love…'

THEO *stands there watching them dance, smirking as* PEADAR *paternally kisses* EMER*'s forehead. He studies* PEADAR*'s beaming face as* EMER *leaves, blowing kisses to* JUNIOR *and waving to them all as she goes.*

Ciao, amigos.

PEADAR *waves her on her way.*

THEO. Joy to the world, hah?

PEADAR. What…? Yeah.

THEO. Image of her sometimes – the way she goes on, like! Where's she stoppin' tonight?

PEADAR. Luke's.

THEO. What did she do with all his stuff after?

PEADAR. Don't know… threw it out – burnt it! Herself and Junior.

THEO. Oh right… Poor Luke, hah!

PEADAR. Mmn…

THEO *ponders, shrugs it all off and fingers a damp spot on the edge of the ring.*

THEO (*looking up at the ceiling*). A bit of a leak there, Peadar, by the looks of it.

PEADAR. I see that.

THEO. Yeah… Here he is now – Lazarus…! O'Murachú!

DEAN (*entering*). I see your man's Merc parked at the end of the lane there. What's-his-name… Paddy Hickey the bookie… Must be keepin' tabs on the proceedin's or some-thin'. Someone said that he was whistlin' 'I Dreamt I Dwelt' as I climbed into the ring last night, yeh know. Put the fuckin' hex on me, he did… What's goin' on?

THEO. We're just puttin' Junior through his paces here.

DEAN. What for?

THEO. What do you think?

DEAN *thinks about it and scoffs.*

JUNIOR. What, you got a problem with that?

DEAN. You're the one with the problem, pal, not me.

JUNIOR. Would you like to come in here and spar me?

DEAN. Wouldn't be me first time.

JUNIOR. No, but I guarantee it'll be your last though.

DEAN *scoffs.*

What?

JUNIOR *stares him out of it.* DEAN *sort of hangs his head and, slightly ruffled, sits down on a nearby bench and is soon engrossed in a boxing magazine.* THEO *and* PEADAR *are impressed by* JUNIOR's *aggression.* PEADAR *puts the gloves on* JUNIOR.

THEO. I see your man changed stance a few times last night, Peadar – from southpaw to orthodox and back again – just like that... You'd want to watch out for that, Peadar.

PEADAR. Yeah.

JUNIOR. Don't worry, he won't try that one on me.

DEAN. How's that then?

JUNIOR. Because I'll knock him out if he does.

DEAN. Ssss... (*Returning to the magazine.*)

JUNIOR. Somethin' funny in there, yeah?

DEAN. I'll say. Not 'alf! Eh?

JUNIOR. Yeh what?

DEAN. Huh?

Dangerous pause.

PEADAR (*mitt on his hand*). Come on, let's go.

JUNIOR *dances in and throws a combination into the mitt,* PEADAR *weaving in and around the ring.*

THEO. Lovely, Junior... That's it, that's the spirit. Go on again now... That's it. Burst into it.

THEO *turns and indicates to* DEAN *his appreciation for* JUNIOR*'s work rate.*

PEADAR. Again. Come on. Keep movin'... That's it. And again... Lovely... Once more... That's it... Move and stick... Move and stick... That's it... Left jab... And again... Double up... Lovely... One more time now... Lovely.

Lights down.

*Lights rise. It is night. The boxing booth is empty. We hear
laughing voices approaching. Soon* EMER *runs on and hides in
the shadows, literally wrapping herself around the punchbag
with her feet off the ground.* JUNIOR *enters, searching for her.
She drops down and playfully swings the big punchbag at him.
He weaves out of the way and catches her, draws her near and
they kiss. Madly in love, he lifts her up onto the side of the ring
and soon joins her there.*

EMER. Did you see him?

JUNIOR (*kissing her all the time*). Who?

EMER. Paddy Hickey the bookie.

JUNIOR. Where?

EMER. Parked at the end of the lane there.

JUNIOR. Yeah?

EMER. Yeah – in his Merc… I wonder what he's up to? This
hour of the night, like… Did you not see him, no?

JUNIOR (*emphatic*). No.

EMER. Uhmmn… (*She returns his kisses.*) I'm supposed to get
you to bed early tonight, yeh know.

JUNIOR. So why don't yeh then?

She slaps his hand lovingly.

EMER. You're meant to be conservin' your energy.

JUNIOR. Yeah?

EMER. Yeah. That bloody aul' fight…! Ahh… me and my…
(*She cringes at the thought of it all.*)

JUNIOR. It's what I do.

EMER. It doesn't have to be. You could do other things.

JUNIOR. Like what?

EMER. I don't know. You could fix things.

JUNIOR. I do – fix things.

EMER. I know, that's what I'm sayin'… If you ask me I think we should get out of here altogether. Just pack our bags and beat it, let them sort out their own mess… Why not? I mean, you don't owe 'em nothin' here. Neither do I for that matter.

JUNIOR. Come on now, you can't be doin' things like that… Anyway I thought you wanted me to fight this bloke?

EMER. Yeah I know but I didn't necessarily envisage you actually… physically… yeh know…

JUNIOR. Don't worry… I'll duck.

EMER. You'd better – duck, weave, bob, whatever, just – you know…

JUNIOR. Hang on. Duck, weave… what was the last one?

He pretends to take a note of it. She turns her back on him in mock disgust.

What? Here… Did yeh hear the one about the corner man who said to the fighter, 'You're doin' good, kid, he's not layin' a glove on yeh.' 'Well,' says the fighter, 'You'd better keep an eye on the referee then because someone's hittin' me.' (*He chuckles.*)

EMER. The referee was hittin' him?

JUNIOR. What? No, he was…

EMER. What? (*She smirks.*)

JUNIOR. Oh right, very funny…

EMER (*pointing a 'got you' finger at him*). Ah!

JUNIOR (*pretending to bite her finger*). Hmn…

A distant train moans.

EMER (*sitting up*). The twelve o'clock milk train. I love that sound. Hear it…? I wish we were on that now, the two of us – get us out of here. Do you hear it?

JUNIOR. Yeah… The driver probably has a big permanent what-d'you-call-it… (*Mimes 'ring around his mouth'.*) Mmn… Daisy Day! (*He smacks his lips.*)

EMER *chortles and leans into him.*

EMER. Yeah… (*She mimes pulling the whistle.*) Moo… Moo.

JUNIOR. All the cows runnin' after it… Moo…

EMER. Come back… come back…

JUNIOR. Moo…

EMER. Ba… Ma…

JUNIOR *acts perplexed.*

…There's goats' milk in the last carriage. Ma…

JUNIOR. Oh right.

EMER. There she goes – through the mountain… (*She makes the sound of a shunting train.*) Goditt goditt goditt goditt goditt… Too late – she's gone and we're stranded! Like poor little lambs…! Tch, I don't know… I never knew the referee could hit yeh.

JUNIOR. Aah…

They laugh and cuddle as she examines his face.

EMER. How did you get that scar there?

JUNIOR. Which one…? Oh… Cardiff – a fella called Richie something or other, Golden – that's it… Yeah – Richie Golden… Gave me a right smack.

EMER. What about that one?

JUNIOR. I got that in the boys' home. Three stitches – fell off a railin'… Broke me thumb too once… that one there… How about you, what's your excuse?

EMER (*slapping him*). The cheek of you…! (*Pause.*) I went down to the Shrine today and said a prayer for yeh… Not that you'd win or lose or anything but that you'd come out of it all alright, in one piece… Not too much to ask for, is it?

JUNIOR. No... As a matter of fact, I think you could have asked for a little more actually – a draw at least!

She pretends to elbow him.

You said a prayer for the other lad too while you were down there, right?

EMER. No... Should I?

He chastises her with a look.

Our Lady'll look after the two of yez.

JUNIOR. Yeh reckon?

EMER. I do.

They kiss.

JUNIOR (*climbing down and approaching the bag*). Yeah well, let's hope so.

He begins to thump the bag, softly at first, and then he puts his head down and pounds it so that EMER *begins to understand the danger ahead. Almost in an attempt to stop it all, or to slow him down at least, she goes to him and snuggles into his back. Lights down.*

Lights rise on the boxing booth. It is Friday afternoon now. JUNIOR, *in a lather of sweat, is punching the big heavy bag which* PEADAR *is holding.* EMER *is sitting close at hand as* LILY *enters with a plate of food in one hand and a glass of milk in the other.*

PEADAR. Head, body, head. That's it. And again. Head, body, head and double up. Lovely... go on again now... Head, body, head... Go on... double up... Lovely stuff. One more time...

LILY. Here y'are, Peadar. Steak and onions, mushrooms and baby potatoes and a glass of Daisy Day – for the fightin' man.

PEADAR. What...? Thanks. That'll do yeh, Junior. Get somethin' inside yeh there now. Take a bit of a nap in the trailer

then and I'll come over and put on the bandages and that
later on – when the time is right... Good. It's good to work
up a bit of a sweat like that... How's the foot?

JUNIOR. Alright. A bit of a twinge, that's all. Should be alright,
I'd say.

JUNIOR *slips off his sweatshirt and begins towelling himself
dry as* PEADAR *looks him over.*

PEADAR. Good... Very good... Yeah... Cup of tea, I think.

PEADAR *takes the boiling teapot and makes the tea and
then places it back on the stove again to draw, and then he
moves about, putting the ropes back into place around the
ring. Meanwhile,* EMER, *absentmindedly, thumbs through a
boxing magazine.* LILY *approaches the punchbag, wrapping
herself around it seductively.*

LILY. Alright, Junior?

JUNIOR. Yeah, I think so.

LILY. You're sweatin'.

JUNIOR. Huh?

LILY. I say you're wringin' wet, boy.

JUNIOR (*breathless*). Yeah, well... (*He signals that it is par for
the course.*)

LILY. Tired?

JUNIOR. I'm alright.

LILY. Yeah...? Here, turn round...

She takes the towel from him and wipes his back, etc.

Yeh know, I was just thinkin' there about the first day you
arrived here amongst us. Little did we all know then, eh?

JUNIOR. What's that?

LILY. What's that, he says...!

She slaps him playfully with the towel.

You're the saviour, boy – sent to save us…! A poor limpin'
stray you were like that day though – torn jeans and denim
jacket and a polka-dot shirt, which you still have, I notice.
Do you fellows ever throw anything out at all? The boxin'
brigade!

PEADAR. Yeh what?

LILY. And there was a note, wasn't there? – Tucked inside your
thing-me-jig… 'Cat Bergin sent me,' or somethin', which for
some reason did the trick. Hired on the spot. Ha…! And here
y'are now – savin' the day! And do you know what? I think
you can do it too.

JUNIOR. Yeh reckon?

LILY. I do. You're goin' to beat him. I know it. I can feel it – in
here.

JUNIOR. I'll have a good go anyway.

LILY. I know you will. (*She smells the towel.*) Mmn… I love
that smell!

*JUNIOR turns to look at her. She becomes coy and flirtatious
with him under EMER's jealous gaze. JUNIOR gently takes
the towel from her, wraps it around his neck and slips on his
fresh polka-dot shirt. He goes across to the table where, after
blessing himself, he slumps over the meal like a hungry
animal. LILY and EMER trade glances.*

*PEADAR comes across to hoist the big bag up out of the
way and to secure the rope to a nearby hook, etc., as EMER
comes closer.*

EMER. What do you think, Peadar? Is he goin' to be alright?

PEADAR. I'd say so. We could have done with a little more
time, mind yeh, but… Should be alright.

EMER. Supposin' somethin' goes wrong though, Peadar – with
his foot or somethin'? 'Cause Junior said he won't lie down
like Dean did, yeh know.

PEADAR. The referee can always call a halt to it.

EMER. Supposin' he doesn't?

PEADAR. Throw in the towel.

EMER. Yeah, will yeh though, Peadar...? Promise me you will
if he runs into trouble. With his foot, I mean... Say you will.

LILY. Nobody's throwin' in the towel. I mean, there's enough
feckin' deadbeats around here already as it is without us
addin' another one to the list. Junior's goin' to win tonight.
He promised me he's goin' to do it. (*She calls across the
room.*) Ain't that right, Junior?

JUNIOR (*over his shoulder*). What's that?

LILY. I say you're goin' to do it tonight. For me!

JUNIOR. I'll give it a good go anyway.

LILY. See.

EMER. For you?

LILY. Yeah, for me... For all of us! So no one's chuckin' in the
towel, right? I mean, come on – Cat Bergin sent him!

LILY *exits, full of fire, tossing* JUNIOR*'s hair on her way
out, much to his chagrin.*

EMER. What's the matter with that one, Peadar? I mean, one
minute she's... I don't know.

PEADAR. She's with Theo, ain't she – what do you expect?

EMER. Yeh what?

PEADAR. It's what he attracts, what he's drawn to.

EMER. What's that supposed to mean?

PEADAR *laughs.*

...What?

PEADAR. That's exactly what your mother would have done
too – jumped up and down like that and then went and hid
out somewhere for a few hours.

EMER. Hid out? Where?

PEADAR. I don't know – a little cubbyhole behind the Ghost
    Train there or somewhere. I'd have to go and entice her out
    before the show. I'd peep in to find her engrossed in some
    book or other, cushions and blankets all around her and a
    wicker basket on her lap. Or she might be writin' a poem
    maybe. In her wee notebook – 'Lay Me Down Softly' or
    something. Big sad eyes on her. I always maintained that
    Joy wasn't her real name at all, yeh know. Couldn't be –
    she cried that much... Ah no, don't get me wrong now or
    anything. I mean, she laughed a fair bit too while she was
    here. 'Cause there was a sort of a skittish side to her as
    well, yeh know. You're very like her in fact, the way you
    go on sometimes.

She smiles.

EMER. You got on well with her then?

PEADAR. Suppose I did... We should never have left her
    behind that time... It was a lousy thing to do.

EMER. At least you went back to look for her anyway. More
    than he did!

PEADAR. To be honest with yeh I didn't expect her to still be
    there. But there she was, sittin' on the veranda of the Sea
    Breeze Hotel, tryin' to come to terms with it all. Lady Day it
    was – I only know that now because it was written in her
    notebook. I sat down beside her and she let fly: tears, recrim-
    inations, blamed herself a little bit and then cursed the lot of
    us into a knot for leavin' her there, called us all sorts of
    things – tinkers, scoundrels and carnival whores. Oh now, it
    was fairly choice. I asked her did she want to go back home
    again or anything, but she didn't. She said she didn't really
    know what that word meant any more – home! So I went in
    and paid her bill and then we got into the truck and I drove
    the opposite way – about forty or fifty mile down the coast in
    the rain. We stopped at a little town for lunch – Love's Café,
    I'll never forget that. Later on I booked her into a B&B over-
    lookin' the harbour. A sad aul' place really – big brass bed
    and empty drawers and a noisy wardrobe full of hangers.
    Through the window you could see the sea. When I opened

the window you could smell it. And when it grew dark you could still sort of... sense it there. Somewhere along the line I nipped out and got some kindling and coal and, although we weren't supposed to, I lit a fire in the grate and she read me one of her poems.

'Wash me and comb me
And lay me down softly
Lay me down softly
At the end of the day...'

Shortly afterwards she fell asleep and when the time was right I covered her up and snuck off for a second time – lousy I know – down the creaky aul' stairs and away. (*He clucks out his last five footsteps. He looks at* EMER *and shrugs.*)

JUNIOR. This tea fresh, Peadar?

PEADAR. What...? Yeah, I just made it there.

JUNIOR. Are yeh wantin' a sup?

PEADAR. Yeah, go on then.

JUNIOR. I always get a terrible thirst on me before a fight, yeh know. Queer, ain't it? Gallons! Of water! And tea! I don't know why.

THEO (*entering*). Peadar, give us out those aul' bandages there, will yeh... Alright, Junior, did yeh get somethin' to eat and all, yeah?

JUNIOR. Yeah.

THEO. What did she give him?

PEADAR. I don't know – steak and onions and mushrooms and that.

THEO. Good. Did you enjoy it, Junior?

JUNIOR. Yeah, it was alright.

THEO. Good man... He'd want to get a bit of rest now, Peadar, I think, a bit of an aul' lie-down for an hour or so.

PEADAR (*rising to root in the drawer of the small table for the roll of bandage*). Yeah, I was just sayin' that to him there. Go over to the trailer, have a bit of a nap and then I'll come over and apply the bandages and that later on – just before the off, like.

THEO. Sounds good to me. What do you think, Junior?

JUNIOR *nods and takes another gulp of tea.*

Your man Dempsey has arrived anyway – and his entourage.

PEADAR. Already?

THEO. He's a pro, Peadar.

PEADAR. Yeah, I know but… for fuck's sake, like…

THEO. I did the deal with him and that. Six rounds, winner takes all. If it's a draw we'll split the purse down the middle. (*Re: the bandages.*) Cut us off a bit there, Peadar, will yeh… A little more… Too much… That's it… He's insistin' on a neutral referee, which I suppose is fair enough; and two of the boys from the local boxin' club'll act as judges. That'll cost us another box of trophies, Peadar, but that's alright, ain't it?

PEADAR. Oh yeah, we've lashings of trophies, sure.

THEO. So, all above-board then. (*He pours himself a quick mug of tea and butters some brack with the back of a spoon.*) He was lookin' for a trailer to change in but I told him he'll have to get ready around the back, the same as the rest of them. Fuck that, Peadar, I'm not goin' to make it handy for him.

DEAN (*entering*). Theo, Joey Dempsey wants to know if he can use his own gloves. I have them here, look.

PEADAR. Show, give us a look.

DEAN *hands* PEADAR *the gloves, which he inspects closely.*

DEAN. Sadie and little Ernie are at each other's throats out there.

THEO (*munching*). What brought that on?

DEAN. Don't ask me. He's not a happy little man anyway –
from what I can gather.

THEO. Business and pleasure, yeh see. Don't go…! (*Re: the
gloves*.) What do you think, Peadar?

PEADAR. Yeah – should be alright.

THEO. What are they? Ten ounce?

PEADAR. Yeah.

THEO. That's alright, ain't it?

PEADAR. I'd prefer twelve, but… Don't matter… Might suit
us actually, come to think of it. (*He gives the gloves to
DEAN.*)

THEO. Fair enough… Tell him I said that'll be alright, subject
to the referee's inspection tell him… Keep him guessin',
Peadar, eh?

PEADAR. That's it.

THEO. Here, do you want to wish Junior good luck before you
go?

DEAN. What?

THEO. I'll say. Not 'alf! Eh?

Laughter – JUNIOR *included.*

DEAN. Oh yeah, right… Very funny… Good luck.

JUNIOR. Thanks. Unfortunately Lady Luck don't come into it
tonight I'm afraid.

DEAN. Want to bet?

JUNIOR. Huh?

DEAN. Do you hear Junior, lads? Luck don't come into it!

JUNIOR. Come again.

DEAN. Believe you me, mate, you'll be prayin' for luck if he hits
you with that double left jab. You'll go down – same I did.

JUNIOR. Like a bag of shit, yeh mean?

DEAN. Fuck you, pal.

THEO. Yup out of that!

PEADAR. Steady now.

DEAN. What?

THEO. Not fuckin' 'alf! Eh?

PEADAR. Oh dear!

DEAN. Yeh what?

JUNIOR. I'll say!

Laughter all round.

DEAN. Junior, I hope he fuckin' brains you in the first fuckin'
round, yeh fuckin'…

THEO. Ah now!

JUNIOR. Lovely!

DEAN. …Yeh fuckin'… gimp, yeh!

PEADAR. Hey, that'll do yeh now.

More laughter from JUNIOR *and* THEO.

DEAN. Yes, half a cripple goin' round, climbin' into the ring
with a real fighter. I mean, it's a joke – has to be.

PEADAR. That'll do yeh, I said. This is neither the time nor
place now to be settlin' old…

DEAN. Who do you think you are, eh Peadar, Jersey fuckin' Joe
or someone?

PEADAR. I don't want Junior upset now, that's all. No more
than I done for you the other night here.

DEAN. Peadar, you're nothing only a washed-out aul' stum-
blebum. I mean, whatever about Junior there but I wouldn't
even lower meself to…

PEADAR. Here, take the gloves, Dean, and go, will yeh, before
you make me say somethin' or do somethin' I'll be sorry for.

DEAN. Yeah? Like what?

PEADAR. Go ahead.

DEAN. Like what I said, Peadar. Hah?

PEADAR. Dean, do yourself a favour now.

DEAN. Fuck you! (*He flings one of the gloves viciously in* PEADAR's *face.*)

THEO. Hey!

PEADAR. Go ahead now.

DEAN. Or what? You'll hit me with your handbag.

PEADAR. I'll hit yeh with somethin'.

DEAN. Fuck you! I come in here and you give this 'I'll say, not fuckin' 'alf' shit. Fuck you, the lot of yez!

JUNIOR (*calmly*). Dean, you're nothin' only a bag of shit and you know it.

DEAN. Bag of what...? Here...

DEAN *flings the remaining glove into* JUNIOR's *face and upends the table with the teapot and empty dinner plate, etc.* PEADAR *makes a move towards him but* THEO – *flinging the mug aside* – *gets there first, catching* DEAN *in a vicious stranglehold.*

THEO. Now you listen to me, me little maneen, don't you even think for one minute, one second even...

DEAN (*in pain*). Ah...!

PEADAR (*concerned*). Theo... Theo... Stop now...

THEO. ...that you even remotely belong in the same category as any of the rest of us here in this room, or this place rather. I mean even remotely, right?

PEADAR. Theo, like a good man, let him go, will yeh.

THEO. 'Cause if you were, you'd be on the floor there now, bleedin' from every orifice...

PEADAR. Theo… Leave it… Let him go now.

EMER (*intervening*). Theo… stop it… Stop it, I said… Peadar, tell him…

PEADAR. Theo… Come on now…

THEO. Right? Got that? Yeah? Point taken?

DEAN (*in pain*). Alright, Theo… Alright, alright…

EMER. Theo…! Junior, tell him…

THEO. You wouldn't even lower yourself, hah…

DEAN. I'm sorry, Theo, I'm sorry.

THEO. 'Sorry, Peadar,' yeh mean?

DEAN. Sorry, Peadar… Sorry.

PEADAR. Alright. You're alright… Theo…

THEO. Now you pick up those gloves, go outside and put on a hat and stand behind the candyfloss machine for the duration, right?

DEAN. Right.

THEO *releases him and* DEAN, *feeling his aching neck, does as he was bid.*

THEO (*calling after him*). Listen, here, take those bandages out to Joey Dempsey on your way… And stay there for the evenin' too… Until I tell you otherwise… Go ahead… Lower yourself!

DEAN *exits.*

What?

EMER. Me heart! I thought you were goin' to kill him there for a minute. I mean, his face was practically…

THEO. Kill him? For throwin' a few gloves around? Are yeh coddin' me or what? What's wrong with you…? Alright, Junior?

JUNIOR (*rising, unmoved by it all*). Yeah, I'll head on over I think.

EMER. Hang on, I'll come with yeh.

JUNIOR. What?

PEADAR. I'll be over shortly, Junior. Sort yeh out then, eh? – with the bandages and that.

JUNIOR. Yeah, right, Peadar.

EMER *and* PEADAR *share a glance.*

THEO. You don't stay too long over there with him now, do yeh hear me?

EMER *makes a face and exits with* JUNIOR. THEO *gives* PEADAR *a hand to finish setting up the ropes.*

...What do you make of her, Peadar?

PEADAR. Emer? Yeah, I'd be fairly fond of her, mind yeh.

THEO. So am I, Peadar, but... Yeh know? (*He throws his hands in the air.*) Mind you, I suppose I didn't see a whole lot of that kind of stuff meself when I was a young fella, so... You're lucky, Peadar. I always said that. Yeh know you're real... I don't know... self-contained or something. 'A proud and lonely creature.' Cat Bergin, hah?

PEADAR (*shyly*). Cat had a way with words alright.

THEO. He did, didn't he? 'A proud and lonely creature'! God only knows what he said about me, of course.

PEADAR. You don't want to know.

THEO. No, I don't suppose I do.

LILY *enters.*

LILY. Your man is winnin' all before on the Rifle Range out there – Buffalo Bill or whatever you call him! Little Ernie's nearly doin' his nut lookin' at him... A rael crack shot altogether he is. Yeah, the FCA, I'd say, definitely...! I don't see Paddy Hickey the bookie out there yet, mind yeh. I thought sure he'd have graced us with his presence by now. Yum yum yum...

THEO *looks at her darkly as she goes into the kiosk.*

THEO (*feeling belittled*). Get us out that aul' megaphone there, Peadar, will yeh.

PEADAR *reaches under the ring for the megaphone.*

(*Calling in to* LILY.) How's that turnstile doin'?

LILY (*off*). I don't know. We'll soon see, won't we?

THEO (*half to himself*). Suppose we will...

He receives the megaphone and looks pensively towards LILY *in the kiosk.*

...It's nearly time here, Peadar, I think.

PEADAR. Yeh reckon?

THEO. I do...

LILY *is singing inside.* THEO – *tormented – looks towards the sound.*

...To tell yeh the truth I don't think I'm cut out for this love lark – somehow or other. It's too... (*He mimes a knife to his guts.*) Yeh know? But what can I do? Nothin'!

He looks to PEADAR *as if for guidance but he gets little or nothing back.*

If you ever see anything goin' on or hear anything goin' on around here you'll let me know, right?

LILY (*off*). Are you wantin' me to go out and buy all the stuff back from this fella later on or what?

THEO. No, let him lug it all home this time, see how he likes that for a change.

LILY (*off*). Cut off your nose, yeh mean...? Maybe we should just put him on the payroll and be done with it, what do you think?

THEO *sighs as* LILY *appears in the doorway with her arms folded.*

Of course, if Peadar was doin' his job right he'd've seen this comin'.

THEO. There was no way Peadar – or anyone else around here eider for that matter – could have known that that fella was a…

LILY. No, but he should have seen him comin' in the gate tonight and ran him out of it, instead of fawnin' over that young one all day every day like she was the answer to everything.

THEO. Hey!

LILY. Jaysus, anyone'd think she was Hayley Mills or someone the way he goes on. Well, let me tell you, mister, she's no Hayley fuckin' Mills… (*She turns to* THEO.) And you'd want to cop on to yourself too – before she cleans yeh out and wipes your eye for yeh. Yes, Hayley fuckin' Mills! Ha!

She disappears back inside again. THEO *sighs and looks to* PEADAR *to indicate that this is precisely what he was talking about. He slowly exits and very soon we hear him bellowing through the megaphone.*

In the meantime, PEADAR *stands and takes a long apprehensive look around. He picks up the roll of bandage and makes to leave.* EMER *enters and tearfully goes to him. He embraces and comforts her.* LILY *begrudgingly watches them from the kiosk.*

THEO (*off, through the megaphone*). Ladies and gentlemen, step this way. The Academy Boxing Booth will soon be open for business. Tickets are on sale as we speak. Come early to avoid disappointment and get the best seats in the house. First come, first served. The Academy will soon be open for business. Get your tickets, my friends, and then go and enjoy the Funfair – the Helter Skelter, the Ghost Train, the Swing Boats and Merry-Go-Round and all the other fairground attractions before ending the evening inside our famous Academy Boxing Hall. Top of the bill tonight we have the incredible Joey Dempsey, local welterweight boxer and one-time champion of the region. In the other corner we have the remarkable and, yes folks, the undefeated Junior Hayes who makes his comeback tonight in the Academy Boxing Hall… What a battle this will be!

Also on the bill, my friends, we have none other than the one and only Peadar Ryan who's going to take on Sergeant Flynn of the 7th Battalion in a winner-takes-all, five-guinea challenge…

Lights down. In the darkness we hear the bell ringing and the roaring crowd and we catch a brief sense of the atmosphere of the big fight.

Lights rise. It is night. PEADAR *is treating* JUNIOR*'s cuts and bruises and washing his wounds and cleaning them and dabbing them with iodine, etc., applying clean plasters where necessary and the odd stitch here and there.* EMER, *who is close by and keeping an eye on the proceedings, winces at the ferocity of the wounds. Her bag is packed and lying at her feet.*

EMER. It's not fair, I'm tellin' yeh. I mean, Junior won that fight fair and square out there tonight. He should have got the decision. I mean, even I could see that.

PEADAR. It don't work like that in a boxing booth, Emer. If a fight goes the distance it's usually deemed a draw – for obvious reasons. And let's face it, your man earned his fair share of the purse there tonight now.

EMER. Yeah and meanwhile what will Junior get out of it? Nothin'.

JUNIOR. I'm on wages though, Emer.

EMER. Pittance, yeh mean.

JUNIOR (*in pain*). Ah…

PEADAR. Hold still for me, will yeh.

JUNIOR. For fuck sake, Peadar.

PEADAR. Nearly there now. Look up to the light… That's it. Put that hand down.

JUNIOR. Jaysus.

PEADAR. I know. Musha musha…

EMER. You should have looked after him in there anyway. You promised me you would and you didn't. You should have threw in the towel like you said you would.

PEADAR. He won, for fuck sake.

EMER. Theo won, yeh mean... (*To* JUNIOR.) I don't want you doin' this any more, do you hear me? I want you to come away with me now and forget about this lark altogether. Get a job, an ordinary job somewhere.

JUNIOR. I have a job... Shit!

PEADAR. Head up and look at me... That's it... You'll live.

JUNIOR. Show, give us a look. (*He reaches for a small mirror.*)

PEADAR (*putting his tools away*). Oh stop, you're lovely...! Who will I leave them to, eh? (*His hands.*)

EMER *sulkily turns away.*

THEO (*entering*). Do you know what, I must have a sign on me or somethin', have I?

PEADAR. How's that?

THEO. That little prick is nearly after cleanin' us out on the Rifle Range again there now. I wouldn't mind but I told him to piss off several times. But no, he kept on shootin'. And don't ask me where Ernie is. Your man Rusty's mindin' the fort out there at the moment. I don't know... Yes, a sign I must have! How's he doin' there? (*He studies* PEADAR*'s handiwork.*) Oh yes, nice job, Peadar. Fair play to yeh. The best cut-man in the business, boy. Hah...? Is that a stitch there, Peadar, yeah?

PEADAR. Yeah, just a... little tuck.

THEO. Neat... So, are yeh all set, yeah?

EMER. Yeah.

THEO. Good. Bags packed, hat and everything, hah!

EMER. Mmn... Don't ask me to stay whatever yeh do!

THEO. Stay if yeh want, up to you, makes no odds to me – one way or another…! I mean… You should hang on till the mornin' at least. I'll get Lily to drop yeh home in the truck. Won't yeh, Lily?

LILY (*entering from the kiosk*). What?

THEO. I say you'll drop Emer home in the mornin' if she hangs on.

LILY. Yeh what?

EMER. It's alright, I'm goin' to cut across the field and catch the milk train.

THEO. Fair enough… How did we do?

> EMER *throws* THEO *a vengeful look as he turns away.*

LILY. Good.

THEO. Show us.

> LILY *hands him the cashbox, brimming with notes and coins. He takes it to the table and sits to count it.*

> Get us out the big ledger there, Lily, will yeh? Here, what do you think of this fella then?

LILY (*going into the kiosk to get the ledger*). Who's that? Junior! Lovely! Beautiful. The man's a warrior. What I saw of it anyway.

THEO. See. And she's a woman! He's after loanin' Joey Dempsey his trailer to change in and everything, yeh know. How's that for sportsmanship?

LILY (*off*). There was nothin' sportsmanlike about that other fella tonight then. A rael mauler he was.

THEO. Ah, you wouldn't mind that – par for the course, that… That was practically a sell-out there tonight, yeh know.

LILY (*returning*). I know.

THEO. I mean, the whole place was talkin' about him goin' out the door.

LILY. I don't blame them... I mean, he gave an exhibition in there tonight. Of manhood! Are yeh alright?

JUNIOR. Yeah.

LILY. You're fairly sore I'd say, are yeh?

JUNIOR. I'm alright.

LILY. Show, give us a look... Let's see... (*She goes to him and begins to massage his shoulders, etc.*) Oh yes... You're stiff... Well, you saved the day like I said you would – our little saviour boy! And I'm goin' to tell one thing now for nothin', Junior, but I'm goin' to see to it that you get all that's comin' to you around here too from now on. Yes, all that's comin' to yeh, boy. Hah? And the rest of yez may get used to it! With your jigsaws and your... Ovaltine! Ha!

She snuggles into him, kisses his neck and giggles. EMER *shuffles uneasily and* JUNIOR *shifts uncomfortably and* PEADAR *seems a little concerned.* THEO *is looking across at it all too, grinning benignly – which is always a bad sign.*

I hope you know what you have on your hands here, mister?

THEO. I do... A gold mine!

LILY *tousles* JUNIOR*'s hair affectionately as* DEAN *enters.*

DEAN. Theo, you better get out here quick – little Ernie's gone berserk over there.

THEO. What's up with him?

DEAN. It seems he caught Sadie and Paddy Hickey the bookie together earlier on there at the end of the lane – in his Mercedes. He was goin' to kill her and everything over it. She's after barricadin' herself into the trailer to get away from him. He's got a big sort of... an iron crowbar now and he's after smashin' all the windows and he's tryin' to break down the door with it.

THEO. What the fuck!

DEAN. I know. She swore she was only there to tell him his fortune, but...

JUNIOR. Probably was.

DEAN. What – on her hands and knees?

JUNIOR. Oh!

DEAN. Yeah.

THEO. I don't know. Just when you think you're gettin' some-where, someone goes and…

LILY. But sure what do you expect when you're a soft touch?

THEO. How do you mean?

LILY. You're a soft touch for 'em all – Peadar and Rusty and Ernie and… (*She indicates* EMER.) A rael pushover if you ask me, a laughing stock if you're not careful!

THEO. A laughin' stock?

LILY. You know what I mean.

THEO. No… I don't… Enlighten me.

LILY (*turning away*). Ah!

THEO. What?

DEAN. Do you hear him? Full of whiskey, of course!

THEO (*rising*). Yeh what?

DEAN. Ernie!

THEO. What about him?

DEAN. I say he's… fairly full out there.

Noises off of smashing glass, etc., as THEO, *with a face of vengeance and suspicious of the others, takes the cashbox and ledger back into the kiosk.*

LILY. That Paddy Hickey is nothin' only a sleeveen anyway.

DEAN. How's that?

LILY. Sadie? Ha…! I wouldn't mind but he winked at me every chance he got – the slimy get!

THEO. Paddy Hickey winked at you…? When?

LILY. All the time.

THEO. How come you never said nothin' to me about that?

LILY. I'm tellin' you now, ain't I? I mean, what are you wantin', a signed affit-davitt or somethin'?

THEO. And did he ever say anything to you?

LILY. Like what?

THEO. I don't know – remarks and that?

LILY. Yeah – the odd time!

THEO. Yeah? Did you know anything about this?

PEADAR. What?

THEO. Paddy Hickey the bookie winkin' at her, every chance he got and sayin' things to her and that – remarks and that?

PEADAR. The first I heard tell of it then... Mind you, if you put in for these things you'll get them, I suppose.

LILY. I didn't... I don't...

PEADAR *sort of hisses and turns away.*

...What are you insinuatin' exactly?

THEO. Yeah, Peadar, come on, if you've got somethin' to say, say it.

PEADAR *puts his hands in the air in surrender.*

(*Stabbing* PEADAR *in the chest with a threatening finger.*) In future you keep me in-fucking-formed about these kind of things, do you hear me?

PEADAR *looks down at the prodding finger and then into* THEO*'s dark and dangerous and slightly drunken gaze, much to* LILY*'s delight.*

...What? You got somethin' to say to me, somethin' you want to tell me? Hah...? No...? Good... Now, come on, get your fuckin' skates on and do your job properly for a change, instead of poncin' around here half the fuckin' night... This little fucker better not start anythin' with me out here now because I tell yeh, I'm in no humour for it.

LILY (*as they go*). I'm goin' to tell you one thing, if Paddy Hickey is still here I'll be puttin' a big rock through his...

DEAN. He's not, he's long gone.

LILY. Sleeveen.

THEO. He'd better be gone. 'Cause I'll up-fuckin'-end him.

They are gone – THEO, LILY, DEAN and a reluctant PEADAR. JUNIOR begins to dress as EMER paces. She makes sure the others are gone and then she goes into the kiosk and comes back out with the cashbox. She takes it to the table and begins to stuff all the notes into her bag and most of the coins into her pockets.

JUNIOR (*pulling on his shirt and jeans*). What are yeh doin'?

EMER. He owes us – big time! Are you comin' with me now or not?

JUNIOR. Jesus, Emer, you can't do that.

EMER. Watch me... Come on or we'll miss the milk train. (*She hurries to a flap which she lifts to squeeze out through.*) Yes or no?

JUNIOR. What?

EMER. Ah! (*Going.*) You know where to find me when you come to your senses.

JUNIOR. My what?

She doubles back to kiss him.

EMER. Yeah – while you still have them.

She pauses to look at him and then hurries away. JUNIOR goes to the flap.

JUNIOR. Emer! Emer!

EMER (*off*). Moo... (*She laughs.*)

JUNIOR. Emer!

EMER (*faintly*). Moo…

JUNIOR (*softly*). Emer!

Pause as JUNIOR *turns to look at the empty cashbox on the ground.* PEADAR *returns.*

PEADAR. I don't know… He's up to ninety out there now. And she's not helpin' matters eider, I don't mind tellin' yeh… Where's she gone? Is she gone, yeah? What's up?

JUNIOR *stares back at him, startled.*

JUNIOR. She's after takin' the money, Peadar.

PEADAR. What? She's not, is she? Shit! She is too.

PEADAR *picks up the cashbox and rattles the handful of coins. He goes to the flap.*

Emer! Emer…!

EMER (*distant*). Moo…

PEADAR. Why didn't you stop her…?

JUNIOR *shrugs.*

She's not goin' to make it. Do you think she'll make it…? This is bad. I mean, this is… Fuck!

JUNIOR. What are we goin' to do, Peadar?

PEADAR. I don't know… (*He thinks about it.*) You'd better go after her. Go with her.

JUNIOR. What?

PEADAR. Get her out of here.

PEADAR *fetches* JUNIOR*'s jacket and brings it to him.*

Here… Go on… See that she gets that train… Go ahead.

JUNIOR. But that makes it look like I took the money, Peadar.

PEADAR. It don't matter who took the money, Junior. Someone's goin' to get hurt here now anyway, so… I don't want them cuts open again.

JUNIOR. I don't know… I mean, this is what I do, Peadar, what I am.

PEADAR. Find somethin' else to do.

JUNIOR. Like what?

PEADAR. What do you want me to say, Junior, that you're Rocky Graciano? You're not… I mean he was a has-been there tonight, Junior. Yeh know…? You beat a has-been… Trust me, start anew. (*Holding the flap open.*) Go on, get out of here… (*Roughly pushes him out.*) Go, will yeh.

JUNIOR *is torn between staying and going.*

JUNIOR. Are you goin' to be alright here, Peadar?

PEADAR. Yeah. Go ahead… go on… Oh, listen here. Puncture as many wheels as you can on your way out there. Here. (*He hands him a spike.*) Go ahead. She's nearly at the Shrine now.

JUNIOR *goes.*

(*Calling after him.*) Make sure yeh… The pick-up… I say the… That's it… Go on now… Leave 'em and… go… Go.

JUNIOR *is gone.* PEADAR *watches him go and then he picks up the empty cashbox and winces at the prospects.*

Shit…

DEAN *soon enters.*

DEAN. Little Ernie's in tears out there. Theo said if he didn't put down the big crowbar he'd wrap it around his neck and post him back forthwith to County Monaghan. Second class, says he…! Although I always thought Ernie came from Cavan meself but there you go… apparently not. (*He looks around.*) Junior gone with her or what?

PEADAR. Yeah.

DEAN. What, all the way, like?

PEADAR. Looks like it.

DEAN. Yeah? Well, what do you know... 'Love is a Many Splendour Thing', hah...! (*He looks down at the empty cashbox.*) What's goin' on?

PEADAR. How do you mean?

DEAN. Where's the money...? They took the money...? I don't believe this... (*He snatches the cashbox from* PEADAR.) They took the fuckin' money. (*Tingling with excitement now, he goes to the flap.*) Well, the robbin' little bitch and bastard anyway... How far are they gone...? I see 'em. He's at the Shrine, she's headin' across the field there, look. See 'em... We'll cut them off at the station... Come on, get the boys.

PEADAR (*restraining him*). Leave 'em.

DEAN. What? Come out of me way, will yeh.

PEADAR. Give 'em time, I said.

DEAN. What do you mean?

PEADAR. Dean, they're catchin' that train.

DEAN. Yeah, right... Peadar, if you don't come out of my way I'm goin' to hit yeh a good slap for yourself.

PEADAR. Yeah?

DEAN. Yeah.

DEAN *tries to push* PEADAR *aside but* PEADAR *stands his ground. They tussle.* PEADAR *throws a beautiful combination of punches and floors* DEAN.

PEADAR. Give them time, I said.

DEAN (*groaning*). You're dead... You're fuckin' dead, boy. When I tell Theo... you're dead.

PEADAR. Yeah, right.

DEAN. Yeh what...? What is it with you and her anyway? I mean, anyone'd think... Ah! (*He feels his aching throat.*)

PEADAR (*goes to the flap and looks out*). ...There she goes – Lady of Spain!

PEADAR *smiles sadly.* DEAN *rises and* PEADAR *turns to look at him.*

DEAN. You're finished here, boy... You're fuckin' done. I mean, I'd feel sorry for yeh, only you asked for it.

PEADAR *chuckles.*

What? Brave boy, hah? We'll see how brave you are in a minute. Yes, we'll see how brave you are then.

PEADAR. Look, just go and do what you have to do, will yeh, and don't be annoyin' me... Oh, and listen, Dean... let's dispense with the kiss.

DEAN *curses under his breath and suddenly stumbles off, calling as he goes.*

DEAN (*off*). Theo... Theo... Rusty, where's Theo...? Theo... THEO.

PEADAR *turns to watch him go and then he moves to the edge of the ring where he sits, rolls a cigarette, lights up and, as the milk train moans in the distance, he waits for them to come and get him. Lights down.*

The End.

A Nick Hern Book

Lay Me Down Softly first published in Great Britain as a paperback original in 2008 by Nick Hern Books Limited, 14 Larden Road, London W3 7ST, in association with the Abbey Theatre, Dublin

Cover image courtesy of the National Fairground Archive UK
Cover designed by Ned Hoste, 2H

Typeset by Nick Hern Books, London
Printed and bound in Great Britain by CPI Antony Rowe, Chippenham, Wiltshire

A CIP catalogue record for this book is available from the British Library

ISBN 978 1 84842 030 4